SHANTY

THE BLACKSMITH

A TALE OF OTHER TIMES

MRS. SHERWOOD

1ˢᵗ WORLD
LIBRARY
Literary Society

Shanty the Blacksmith

Mrs. Sherwood

© 1st World Library, 2008
PO Box 2211
Fairfield, IA 52556
www.1stworldlibrary.com
First Edition

LCCN: 2007935423

Softcover ISBN: 978-1-4218-9362-4
Hardcover ISBN: 978-1-4218-9462-1
eBook ISBN: 978-1-4218-9262-7

Purchase *"Shanty the Blacksmith"*
as a traditional bound book at:
www.1stWorldLibrary.com/purchase.asp?ISBN=978-1-4218-9362-4

1st World Library is a literary, educational organization dedicated to:

- Creating a free internet library of downloadable ebooks

- Hosting writing competitions and offering book publishing scholarships.

1st World Library Literary Society

Giving Back to the World

"If you want to work on the core problem, it's early school literacy."

- James Barksdale, former CEO of Netscape

"No skill is more crucial to the future of a child, or to a democratic and prosperous society, than literacy."

- Los Angeles Times

"Literacy... means far more than learning how to read and write... The aim is to transmit... knowledge and promote social participation."

- UNESCO

"Literacy is not a luxury, it is a right and a responsibility. If our world is to meet the challenges of the twenty-first century we must harness the energy and creativity of all our citizens."

- President Bill Clinton

"Parents should be encouraged to read to their children, and teachers should be equipped with all available techniques for teaching literacy, so the varying needs and capacities of individual kids can be taken into account."

- Hugh Mackay

It was during the last century, and before the spirit of revolution had effected any change in the manners of our forefathers, that the events took place, which are about to be recorded in this little volume.

At that period there existed in the wild border country, which lies between England and Scotland, an ancient castle, of which only one tower, a few chambers in the main building, certain offices enclosed in high buttressed walls, and sundry out-houses hanging as it were on those walls, yet remained. This castle had once been encircled by a moat which had been suffered to dry itself up, though still the little stream which used to fill it when the dams were in repair, murmured and meandered at the bottom of the hollow, and fed the roots of many a water plant and many a tree whose nature delights in dank and swampy soils. The verdure, however, which encircled this ancient edifice, added greatly to the beauty, when seen over the extent of waste and wild in which it stood. There can be no doubt but that the ancient possessors of this castle, which, from the single remaining barrier, and the name of the family, was called Dymock's tower, had been no other than strong and dangerous free-booters, living on the plunder of the neighbouring kingdom of Scotland. Every one knows that a vast extent of land, waste or at best but rudely cultivated, had once belonged to the Lords of Dymock; but within a few years this family had fallen from affluence, and were at length so much reduced, that the present possessor could hardly support himself in any thing like the state in which he deemed it necessary for his father's son to live. Mr. Dymock was nearly thirty years of age, at the time our history commences; he had been brought up by an indolent father, and an aunt in whom no great trusts had been vested, until he entered his teens, at which time he was sent to Edinburgh to attend the classes in the college; and there, being a quick and clever young man, though without any foundation of early discipline, or good teaching, and without much plain judgment or common sense, he distinguished himself as a sort of genius.

One of the most common defects in the minds of those who are not early subjected to regular discipline is, that they have no perseverance; they begin one thing, and another thing, but never carry anything on to any purpose, and this was exactly the case with Mr. Dymock. Whilst he was in Edinburgh he had thought that he would become an author; some injudicious persons told him that he might succeed in that way, and he began several poems, and two plays, and he wrote parts of several treatises on Mathematics, and Physics, and Natural History; the very titles of these works sound clever, but they were never finished. Dymock was nearly thirty when his father died; and when he came to reside in the tower, his mind turned altogether to a new object, and that was cultivating the ground, and the wild commons and wastes all around him: and if he had set to work in a rational way he might have done something, but before he began the work he must needs invent a plough, which was to do wonderful things, and, accordingly, he set to work, not only to invent this plough, but to make it himself, or rather to put it together himself, with the help of a carpenter and blacksmith in the neighbourhood. But before we introduce the old blacksmith, who is a very principal person in our story, we must describe the way in which Mr. Dymock lived in his tower.

His aunt, Mrs. Margaret Dymock, was his housekeeper, and

Mrs. Sherwood

so careful had she always been, for she had kept house for her brother, the late laird, that the neighbours said she had half-starved herself, in order to keep up some little show of old hospitality. In truth, the poor lady was marvellously thin, and as sallow and gaunt as she was thin. Some old lady who had stood for her at the font, in the reign of Charles the Second, had, at her death, left her all her clothes, and these had been sent to Dymock's tower in several large chests. Mrs. Margaret was accordingly provided for, for life, with the addition of a little homespun linen, and stockings of her own knitting; but, as she held it a mighty piece of extravagance to alter a handsome dress, she wore her godmother's clothes in the fashion in which she found them, and prided herself not a little in having silks for every season of the year. Large hoops were worn in those days, and long ruffles, and sacks short and long, and stomachers, and hoods, and sundry other conceits, now never thought of; but Mrs. Margaret thought that all these things had a genteel appearance, and showed that those who bought them and those who inherited them had not come of nothing.

Mrs. Margaret, however, never put any of these fine things on, till she had performed her household duties, looked into every hole and corner in the offices, overlooked the stores, visited the larder, scullery and hen-yard, weighed what her three maids had spun the day before, skimmed the milk with her own hands, gathered up the candle ends, and cut the cabbage for the brose; all which being done, and the servants' dinner seen to, and it must be confessed, it was seldom that they had a very sumptuous regale, she dressed herself as a lady should be dressed, and sate down to her darning, which was her principal work, in the oval window in the chief room in the castle. Darning, we say, was her principal work, because there was scarcely an article in the house which she did not darn occasionally, from the floor-cloth to her own best laces, and, as money was seldom forthcoming for renewing any of the finer articles in the house capable of being darned, no one can say what would have been the consequence, if Mrs. Margaret had been divested of this darning propensity.

How the old lady subsisted herself is hardly known, for it often happened that the dinner she contrived for her nephew, was barely sufficient for him, and although on these occasions she always managed to seem to be eating, yet had Mr. Dymock had his eyes about him, he could not but have seen that she must often have risen from the table, after having known little more than the odour of the viands. Nothing, however, which has been said of Mrs. Margaret Dymock goes against that which might be said with truth, that there was a fund of kindness in the heart of the venerable spinster, though it was sometimes choked up and counteracted by her desire to make a greater appearance than the family means would allow.

Besides the three maids in the kitchen, there were a man and a boy without doors, two or three lean cows, a flock of sheep which were half starved on the moor, a great dog, and sundry pigs and fowls living at large about the tower; and, to crown our description, it must be added, that all the domestic arrangements which were beyond the sphere of Mrs. Margaret were as ill managed as those within her sphere were capitally well conducted; however, as Mr. Dymock said to her one day when she ventured to expostulate with him on this subject, "Only have a little patience, my good aunt, when I have completed what I am now about, for instance my plough, you will see how I will arrange every thing. I cannot suffer these petty attentions and petty reforms to occupy me just now; what I intend to do will be done in a large way; I mean not only to repair but to restore the castle, to throw the whole of my lands to the north into a sheep-walk, to plant the higher points, and to convert the south lands into arable. But

Mrs. Sherwood

my first object is the plough, and that must be attended to, before everything else; the wood-work is all complete, but a little alteration must be made in the coulter, and after all, I apprehend I must do it myself, as old Shanty is as stupid as his own hammer."

Mrs. Margaret hinted that every man had not the ingenuity of her nephew; adding, however, that old Shanty was as worthy and God-fearing a man as any on the moor.

"I do not deny it," replied Mr. Dymock, "but what has worth and God-fearing to do with my plough. I have been trying in vain to make him understand what I want done, and am come to the resolution of going myself, taking off my coat, and working with him; I should make a better blacksmith in a week, than he has in forty years."

Mrs. Margaret lifted up her hands and eyes, and then fetching a deep sigh, "That I should have lived to hear that," she exclaimed; "the last representative of the house of Dymock proposing to work at a blacksmith's forge!"

"And why not? Mrs. Margaret," replied the nephew, "does a gentleman lower himself when he works merely for recreation, and not for sordid pelf; you have heard of Peter the Great?"

"Bless me, nephew," replied the spinster, bridling, "where do you think my ears have been all my life, if I never heard of Peter the Great!"

"You know then, that he worked with his own hands at a blacksmith's forge," returned the nephew.

"I know no such thing," said Mrs. Margaret, "and if the Romans say so, I account it only another of their many lies;

and I wonder they are not ashamed to invent tales so derogo-tary to the honour of him they call their head!"

"Pshaw!" said the laird; "I am not speaking of the Pope, but of the Czar of all the Russias!"

"Well! well! Dymock;" returned Mrs. Margaret, "I only wish that I could persuade you from committing this derogation. However, if you must needs work with Shanty, let me beg you to put on one of your old shirts; for the sparks will be sure to fly, and there will be no end of darning the small burns."

"Be assured aunt," said Mr. Dymock, "that I shall do nothing by halves; if I work with Shanty, I shall put on a leathern apron, and tuck up my sleeves."

"All this does not suit my notions," replied Mrs. Margaret: but her nephew had risen to leave her, and there was an end to the argument.

As Mr. Dymock had told his aunt; so he did: he went to Shanty's forge, he dressed himself like the old master himself, and set fairly to work, to learn the mysteries of the trade; mysteries which, however, as far as Shanty knew them, were not very deep.

There has not often been a more ill-arranged and unsettled mind than that of Mr. Dymock; his delight was in anything new, and for a few days he would pursue this novelty with such eagerness, that during the time he seemed to forget every thing else. It was a delicate job, and yet one requiring strength which was needed for the plough. Shanty had told the laird at once, that it was beyond his own skill or strength, seeing that he was old and feeble, "and as to your doing it, sir," he said, "who cannot yet shape a horse-shoe! you must serve longer than a week, before you get that much knowledge of the craft; there is no royal way to learning, and even for the making of a horse-shoe a 'prenticeship must be served, and I mistake me very much if you don't tire before seven days service are over, let alone as many years."

But, Mr. Dymock had as yet served only two days, when one evening a young man, a dark, athletic, bold-looking youth, entered the blacksmith's shed. It was an evening in autumn, and the shed was far from any house; Dymock's tower was the nearest, and the sun was already so low that the old keep with its many mouldering walls, and out-buildings, was seen from the shed, standing in high relief against the golden sky. As the young man entered, looking boldly about him, Shanty asked him what he wanted.

"I want a horse-shoe," he replied.

"A horse-shoe!" returned the blacksmith, "and where's your horse?"

"I has no other horse than Adam's mare," he replied; "I rides no other, but I want a horse-shoe."

"You are a pretty fellow," returned Shanty "to want a horse-shoe, and to have never a horse to wear him."

"Did you never hear of no other use for a horse-shoe, besides protecting a horse's hoof?" replied the youth.

"I have," returned the blacksmith, "I have heard fools say, that neither witch nor warlock can cross a threshold that has a horse-shoe nailed over it. But mind I tell you, it must be a cast shoe."

"Well" said the young man, "suppose that I am plagued with

one of them witches; and suppose that I should have bethought me of the horse-shoe, what would you think of me then? What may that be which you are now shaping; why may it not serve my turn as well as another? so let me have it, and you shall have its worth down on the nail."

"Did not I tell you," said Shanty, sullenly, "that it must be a cast shoe that must keep off a witch; every fool allows that."

"Well," said the young man, looking about him, "have you never a cast shoe?"

"No," replied Shanty, "I have none here fit for your turn."

"I am not particular," returned the young man, "about the shoe being an old one; there is as much virtue, to my thinking, in a new one; so let me have that you are about."

"You shall have none of my handiworks, I tell you," said Shanty, decidedly, "for none of your heathenish fancies and follies. The time was when I lent myself to these sort of follies, but, thank my God, I have learned to cast away, aye, and to condemn such degrading thoughts as these. Believe me, young man, that if God is on your side, neither witch nor warlock, or worse than either, could ever hurt you."

"Well," said the young man, "if you will not make me one, will you let me make one for myself?"

"Are you a smith?" said Mr. Dymock, before Shanty could reply.

"Am I a smith?" answered the young man; "I promise you, I should think little of myself if I was not as much above him, (pointing to Shanty, who was hammering at his horse-shoe, with his back towards him,) as the sun is brighter than

Mrs. Sherwood

the stars."

Shanty took no notice of this piece of insolence; but Mr. Dymock having asked the stranger a few more questions, proceeded to show him the job he wanted done to his plough, and from one thing to another, the young man undertook to accomplish it in a few hours, if the master of the shed would permit. Shanty did by no means seem pleased, and yet could not refuse to oblige Mr. Dymock; he, however, remarked, that if the coulter was destroyed, it was no odds to him. The young stranger, however, soon made it appear that he was no mean hand at the work of a blacksmith; he had not only strength, but skill and ingenuity, and in a short time had so deeply engaged the attention of Dymock by his suggestions of improvements to this same plough, that the young laird saw none but him, and allowed the evening to close in, and the darkness of night to cover the heath, whilst still engaged in talking to the stranger, and hearkening to his ingenious comments on the machinery of the plough.

In the meantime, although the sun had set in golden glory, dark and dense clouds had covered the heavens, the wind had risen and whistled dismally over the moor, and a shower of mingled rain and sleet blew into the shed, one side of which was open to the air. It was in the midst of this shower, that a tall gaunt female, covered with a ragged cloak, and having one child slung on her back, and another much older in her hand, presented herself at the door of the shed, and speaking in a broad northern dialect, asked permission to shelter herself and her bairns, for a little space in the corner of the hut. Neither Dymock nor the young man paid her any regard, or seemed to see her, but Shanty made her welcome, and pointing to a bench which was within the glow of the fire of the forge, though out of harm's way of sparks or strokes, the woman came in, and having with the expertness of long use, slung the child from her back into her arms, she sate down, laying the little one across her knee, whilst the eldest of the two children dropped on the bare earth with which the shed was floored, and began nibbling a huge crust which the mother put into his hand.

In the meantime, work went on as before the woman had come in, nor was a word spoken, till Shanty, looking up from the horse-shoe which he was hammering, remarked in his own mind, that he wondered that the little one stretched on the woman's knee, was not awakened and frightened by the noise of the forge; but there the creature lies, he thought, as if it had neither sense or hearing. When this strange thought suggested itself, the old man dropped his hammer, and fixing his eye on the infant, he seemed to ask himself these questions,—What, if the child should be dead? would a living child, drop as that did from the back of the woman on her lap, like a lump of clay, nor move, nor utter a moan, when thrown across its mother's lap? Urged then by anxiety, he left his anvil, approached the woman, and stood awhile gazing at the child, though unable for some minutes to satisfy himself, or to put away the horrible fear that he might perchance be looking at a body without life. Mr. Dymock was acting the part of bellows-blower, in order to assist some work which the young stranger was carrying on in the fire. The lad who generally performed this service for Shanty, had got permission for a few hours, to visit his mother over the Border, Mr. Dymock having told him in all kindness that he would blow for him if needs must. But the fitful light—the alternate glow and comparative darkness which accompanied and kept time with the motion of the bellows, made it almost impossible for the old man to satisfy himself concerning his horrible imagination. He saw that the infant who lay so still on the woman's lap, was as much as two years of age; that, like the woman, it had dark hair, and that its complexion was olive; and thus he was put out in his first notion, that the child might perchance be a stolen one. But the bellows had

Mrs. Sherwood

filled and exhausted themselves many times before his mind was set at rest with regard to his first fearful thought; at length, however, the child moved its arm, and uttered a low moan, though without rousing itself from its sleep; on which Shanty, being satisfied, turned back to his block and his horse-shoe, and another half-hour or more passed, during which the tempest subsided, the clouds broke and began to disappear, and the stars to come forth one by one, pointing out the direction of the heavens to the experienced eye of the night-walking traveller. The woman observing this, arose, and taking the sleeping babe in her arms whilst the other child clung to her cloak, she thanked the blacksmith for the convenience of the shelter which he had given her; when he, with the courtesy of one who, though poor and lowly, had been admitted to high conference with his Redeemer, invited her to stay longer—all night if she pleased,—regretting only that he had nothing to offer her but a bed of straw, and a sup of sowens for the little ones.

"For which," she replied, "I thank you; what can any one give more than what he has. But time is precious to me, this night I must be over the Border; mind me, however, I shall remember you, and mayhap may call again." So saying, she passed out of the shed, almost as much disregarded by Dymock in her going out, as she had been in coming in.

And now, for another hour, the strokes of the hammers of old Shanty and the young stranger might have been heard far over the moor in the stillness of the night, for the wind had entirely died away, and the fitful glare of the forge, still shone as a beacon over the heath. At length, however, the job which the stranger had undertaken was finished, and Dymock, having given him a silver piece, the only one in his pocket, the young man took his leave, saying as he went out, and whilst he tossed the silver in his hand,—"Well, if I have not got what I came for, I have got that which is as good, and in return for your civility, old gentleman," he added, addressing Shanty, "I give you a piece of advice; nail the horse-shoe, which you would not spare to me, over your own door, for I tell you, that you are in no small danger of being over-reached by the very warlock, who has haunted my steps for many a day."

So saying, he went gaily, and with quick step, out of the shed, and his figure soon disappeared in a ravine or hollow of the moor.

In the mean time, Dymock and Shanty stood at the door. The former being full of excitement, respecting the wonderful sagacity of the singular stranger, and the other being impatient to see the master off, as he wanted to shut up his shed, and to retire to the little chamber within, which served him for sleeping apartment, kitchen, and store-room, not to say study, for our worthy Shanty never slept without studying the Holy Word of God.

But whilst these two were standing, as we said, at the door, suddenly, a low moan reached their ears, as coming from their left, where the roof of the shed being lengthened out, afforded shelter for any carts, or even, on occasion, waggons, which might be brought there, for such repairs as Shanty could give them. At that time, there was only one single cart in the shed, and the cry seemed to come from the direction of this cart. Dymock and Shanty were both startled at the cry, and stood in silence for a minute or more, to ascertain if it were repeated. Another low moan presently ensued, and then a full outcry, as of a terrified child. Dymock and Shanty looked at each other, and Shanty said, "It is the beggar woman. She is still skulking about, I will be bound; hark!" he added, "listen! she will be stilling the child, she's got under the cart." But the child continued to screech, and there was neither threat nor blandishment used to still the cries.

Mrs. Sherwood

Dymock seemed to be so thoroughly astounded, that he could not stir, but Shanty going in, presently returned with a lighted lanthorn, and an iron crow-bar in his hand; "and now," he said, "Mr. Dymock, we shall see to this noise," and they both turned into the out-building, expecting to have to encounter the tall beggar, and with her perhaps, a gang of vagrants. They, however, saw only the infant of two years' old, who had lain like a thing dead on the woman's lap, though not dead, as Shanty had feared, but stupified with hollands, the very breath of the baby smelling of the spirit when Dymock lifted it out of the cart and brought it into the interior shed. Shanty did not return, till he had investigated every hole and corner of his domain, with the crow-bar in one hand, and the lanthorn in the other.

The baby had ceased to cry, when brought into the shed, and feeling itself in the arms of a fellow-creature, had yielded to the influence of the liquor, and had fallen again into a dead sleep, dropping back on the bosom of Mr. Dymock.

"They are all off," said Shanty, as he entered the house, "and have left us this present. We have had need, as that young rogue said, of the horse-shoe over our door. We have been over-reached for once; that little one is stolen goods, be sure, Mr. Dymock,—some great man's child for aught we know,— the wicked woman will not call again very soon, as she promised, and what are we to do with the child? Had my poor wife been living, it might have done, but she is better off! What can I do with it?"

"I must take it up to the Tower," said Mr. Dymock, "and see if my aunt Margaret will take to it, and if she will not, why, then there are charity schools, and poor-houses to be had recourse to; yet I don't fear her kind heart."

"Nor I neither, Mr. Dymock," said Shanty, and the old man

drew near to the child, and holding up his lanthorn to the sleeping baby, he said, "What like is it? Gipsy, or Jew? one or the other; those features, if they were washed, might not disgrace Sarah or Rachel."

"The mouth and the form of the face are Grecian," said Dymock, "but the bust is oriental."

Shanty looked hard at his patron, as trying to understand what he meant by *oriental* and *Grecian;* and then repeated his question, "Gipsy or Jew, Mr. Dymock? for I am sure the little creature is not of our northern breed."

"We shall see by and bye," said Dymock, "the question is, what is to be done now? I am afraid that aunt Margaret will look prim and stately if I carry the little one up to the Tower; however, I see not what else to do. Who is afraid? But put your fire out, Shanty, and come with us. You shall carry the bantling, and I will take the lanthorn. Mayhap, aunt Margaret may think this arrangement the more genteel of the two. So let it be."

And it was so; old Shanty turned into child-keeper, and the Laird into lanthorn-carrier, and the party directed their steps towards the Tower, and much talk had they by the way.

Now, as we have said before, there was a fund of kindness in the heart of Mrs. Margaret Dymock, which kindness is often more consistent than some people suppose, with attention to economy, especially when that economy is needful; and moreover, she had lately lost a favourite cat, which had been, as she said, quite a daughter to her. Therefore the place of pet happened to be vacant just at that time, which was much in favour of the forlorn child's interests. Dymock had taken Shanty with him into the parlour, in which Mrs. Margaret sat at her darning; and he had suggested to the old man, that he might just as well tell the story himself for his aunt's information, and account for the presence of the infant; and, in his own words, Mrs. Margaret took all very well, and even did not hint that if her nephew had been in his own parlour, instead of being in a place where vagrants were sheltered, he would at all events have been out of this scrape. But the little one had awoke, and had begun to weep, and the old lady's heart was touched, so she called one of the maids, and told her to feed the babe and put it to sleep; after which, having ordered that Shanty should be regaled with the bladebone of a shoulder of mutton, she withdrew to her room to think what was next to be done.

The result of Mrs. Margaret's thoughts were, that come what might, the child must be taken care of for a few days, and must be washed and clothed; and, as the worthy lady had ever had the habit of laying by, in certain chests and boxes piled on each other in her large bed-room, all the old garments of the family not judged fitting for the wear of cottagers, she had nothing more to do than, by the removal of half-a-dozen trunks, to get at a deal box, which contained the frocks, and robes, and other garments which her nephew had discarded when he put on jacket and trousers. From these she selected one of the smallest suits, and they might have been seen airing at the kitchen fire by six o'clock that morning. Hot water and soap were next put in requisition, and as soon as the baby awoke, she was submitted to such an operation by the kitchen fire, as it would appear she had not experienced for a long time. The little creature was terribly frightened when soused in the water, and screeched in a pitiful manner; the tears running from her eyes, and the whole of her small person being in a violent tremor. The maids, however, made a thorough job of it, and scoured the foundling from head to foot. At length Mrs. Margaret, who sat by, directing the storm, with a sheet across her lap and towels in her hand, pronounced the ablution as being complete, and the babe was lifted from the tub, held a moment to drip, and then set on the lap of the lady, and now the babe seemed to find instant relief. The little creature was no sooner placed on Mrs. Margaret's knee, than, by some strange and unknown association, she seemed to think that she had found an old friend,—some faintly remembered nurse or mother,—whom she had met again in Mrs. Dymock, and quivering with delight, she sprang on her feet on the lady's lap, and grasped her neck in her arms, pressing her little ruby lips upon her cheek; and on one of the maids approaching again with some of her clothes, she strained her arms more closely round Mrs. Margaret, and perfectly danced on her lap with terror lest she should be taken away from her.

"Lord help the innocent babe!" said the old lady, "what is come to her?" and Mrs. Margaret's eyes were full of tears; but the good lady then soothed and carressed the babe, and instructed her to sit down on her knees, whilst she directed the servant to assist in dressing her. But no, no, it would not do; no one was to touch her but Mrs. Margaret; and the old lady, drawing herself up, at length said,—"Well, Janet, we must give way, I suppose; it seems that I am to be the favourite; there is something in my physiognomy which has taken the child's fancy; come, hand me the clothes, I must try my skill in dressing this capricious little dame." Mrs. Margaret was evidently pleased by the poor orphan's preference, and whilst she was dressing the infant, there was time to discover that the little child was a perfect beauty in her way; the form of her face being oval, the features exquisite, the eyes soft, yet sparkling, and the lips delicately formed. The hair, of raven black, was clustered and curling, and the head set on the shoulders in a way worthy of the daughters of kings; but the servants pointed out on the arm of the infant, a peculiar mark which was not natural, but which had evidently been burnt therein. One said it was a fan, and another a feather; but Mrs. Margaret augured vast things from it, pronouncing that the child surely belonged to some great person, and that no one could say what might be the consequence of kindness shown to such a child.

As soon as Mr. Dymock came down into the breakfast-room, Mrs. Margaret came swimming in with the child in her arms, exclaiming, "A pretty piece of work you have done for me, nephew! I am under a fine servitude now;" and she primmed up her mouth, but her eye laughed,—"little Miss here, chooses to be waited on by me, and me only; and here I am, with nothing to do but to attend on my lady."

"Little Miss," said Mr. Dymock, "what little Miss? who have you got there?"

"Neither more nor less," replied Mrs. Margaret, "than your foundling."

"Impossible!" said Mr. Dymock: "Why, what have you done to her?"

"Merely washed, combed, and dressed her," said Mrs. Margaret; "give me credit, nephew, and tell me what I have brought out by my diligence."

"You have brought out a brilliant from an unfinished stone," exclaimed Mr. Dymock; "that is a beautiful child; I shall have extreme delight in making as much of that fine mind, as you have done with that beautiful exterior."

"Then you do not think of putting her in a foundling hospital or a workhouse, nephew, as you proposed last night?" said Mrs. Margaret, with a smile.

"It would be a folly," replied the nephew, "to degrade such a creature as that;" and he attempted to kiss the baby; but, swift as thought, she had turned her face away, and was clinging to Mrs. Margaret.

The old lady primmed up again with much complacency, "Did I not tell you, nephew, how it was," she said, "nothing will do but Aunt Margaret. Well, I suppose I must give her my poor pussy's corner in my bed. But now her back is turned to you, Dymock, observe the singular mark on her shoulder, and tell me what it is?"

Mr. Dymock saw this mark with amazement:—He saw that it was no natural mark; and at length, though not till after he had examined it many times, he made it out, or fancied he had done so, to be a branch of a palm tree. From the first he had made up his mind that this was a Jewish child; and, following the idea of the palm-tree, and tracing the word in a Hebrew lexicon,—for he was a Hebrew scholar, though not a deep one,—he found that Tamar was the Hebrew for a palm tree. "And Tamar it shall be," he said; "this maid of Judah, this daughter of Zion shall be called Tamar;" and he carried his point, although Mrs. Margaret made many objections, saying it was not a Christian name, and therefore not proper for a child who was to be brought up as a Christian. However, as Mr. Dymock had given up his whim of learning the business of a smith since the adventure which has been so fully related, and had forgotten the proposed experiment of turning up the whole moor round the Tower with his new-fangled plough,—that plough having ceased to be an object of desire to him as soon as it was completed,—she thought it best to give way to this whim of giving the child so strange a name, and actually stood herself at the font, as principal sponsor for little Tamar.

Thus, the orphan was provided with a happy home; nor, as Mrs. Margaret said, did she ever miss the child's little bite and sup. After a few days, the babe would condescend to leave Mrs. Margaret, when required to go to the servants. She would even, when directed so to do, steal across the floor, and accept a seat on Mr. Dymock's knee, and gradually she got very fond of him. Nor was her affection unrequited; he had formed a theory about her,—and it was not a selfish theory, for he never expected to gain anything by her,—but he believed that she was of noble but unfortunate Jewish parentage, and he built this theory on the singular grace and beauty of her person. At all events, he never doubted but that she was a Jewess; and he talked of it, and thought of it, till he was entirely convinced that it was so, and had convinced his aunt also, and established the persuasion in the minds of most persons about him.

If Mr. Dymock was not a genius, he had all the weaknesses commonly attributed to genius, and, in consequence, was as useless a being as ever cumbered the ground; yet, he was generally loved, and no one loved him more than Tamar did, after she had got over her first baby fear of him. But Mrs. Margaret, who had no pretensions to genius, was the real benefactor of this child, and as far as the lady was concerned in bringing her up, performed the part of a truly affectionate mother. Her first effort was made to bring the will of the child, which was a lofty one, under subjection to her own; and the next, to give her habits of industry and self-denial. She told her that whatever she might hear respecting her supposed parentage, she was merely a child without pretentions, and protected from motives of love, and of love only; that her protectors were poor, and ever likely to remain so, and that what God required of her, was that when able, she should assist them as they had assisted her in helpless infancy. As to religion, Mrs. Margaret taught her what she herself knew and believed; but her views were dark and incomplete, she saw not half as much of the great mystery of salvation, as had been revealed to Shanty in his hut; yet, the desire of doing right in the sight of God, had been imparted to her, and this desire was a fixed principle, and did not appear to be affected by her want of knowledge. As to forms, Mrs. Margaret had her own, and she was very attentive to them, but she had very small opportunity of public worship, as there was no church within some miles of the Tower. In the meantime, whilst the old lady went plodding on in her own quiet way, teaching the little girl all she knew herself, Mr. Dymock was planning great things by way of instruction for Tamar. He was to teach her to read her native language, as he called the Hebrew, and to give her various accomplishments, for he had dipped into innumerable branches, not only of the sciences, but of the arts; and as he happened to have met with a mind in Tamar which was as rapid as his own, though far more plodding and persevering, the style of teaching which he gave her, produced far richer fruit than could possibly have been expected. But as Rome was not built in a day, neither must it be supposed that good Mrs. Margaret had not many a laborious, if not weary hour before her part of the care necessary to the well-rearing of the child, was so complete that the worthy woman might sit down and expect a small return; for, as she was wont to say, the child could not be made, for years after she could hold a needle, to understand that the threads should not be pulled as tight in darning as in hem stitch, and this, she would say, was unaccountable, considering how docile the child was in other matters; and, what was worst of all, was this,—that the little girl, who was as wild and fleet, when set at liberty, as a gazelle of the mountains, added not unseldom to the necessity of darning, until Mrs. Margaret bethought herself of a homespun dress in which Tamar was permitted to run and career during all hours of recreation in the morning, provided she would sit quietly with the old lady in an afternoon, dressed like a pretty miss, in the venerable silks and muslins which were cut down for her use when no longer capable of being worn by Mrs. Margaret. By this arrangement Tamar gained health during one part of the day, and a due and proper behaviour at another; and, as her attachment to Mrs. Margaret continued to grow with her growth, many and sweet to memory in after-life were the hours she spent in childhood, seated on a stool at the lady's feet, whilst she received lessons of needlework, and heard the many tales which the old lady had to relate. Mrs. Margaret having led a life without adventures, had made up their deficiency by being a most graphic recorder of the histories of others; Scheherazade herself was not a more amusing story-teller; and if the Arabian Princess had recourse to genii, talismans, and monsters, to adorn her narratives, neither was Mrs. Dymock without her marvellous apparatus; for she had her ghosts, her good people, her dwarfs, and dreadful visions of second sight, wherewith to embellish her histories. There was a piety too, a reference in all she said to the pleasure and will of a reconciled God, which added great charms to her narratives, and rendered them peculiarly interesting to the little girl. Whilst Tamar was under her seventh year, she never rambled beyond the moat alone; but being seven years old, and without fear, she extended her excursions, and not unseldom ran as far as Shanty's shed.

The old man had always taken credit to him self for the part he had had in the prosperity of the little girl, and Mrs. Margaret did not fail to tell her how she had first come to the Tower in Shanty's arms; on these occasions the child used to say,—"then I must love him, must not I ma'am?" And being told she must, she did so, that is, she encouraged the feeling; and on a Sunday when he was washed and had his best coat on, she used to climb upon his knees, for she always asked leave to visit him on that day if he did not come up to the Tower, as he often did, to ask for her, and being on his knees she used to repeat to him what she had been learning during the week.

He was very much pleased, when she first read a chapter in the Bible, and then it was that he first opened out to her some of his ideas on religion; which were much clearer and brighter than either Mrs. Margaret's or her nephew's. How this poor and solitary old man had obtained these notions does not appear; he could not have told the process himself, though, as he afterwards told Tamar, all the rest he knew, had seemed to come to him, through the clearing and manifestation of one passage of Scripture, and this passage was COL. iii. 11. "But Christ is all."

"This passage," said the old man, "stuck by me for many days. I was made to turn it about and about, in my own mind, and to hammer it every way, till at length, I was made to receive it, in its fulness. Christ I became persuaded, is not all to one sort of men, and not all to another sort, nor all at one time of a man's life, and not all at another; nor all in one circumstance of need, and not all in another; nor all to the saints and not all to the sinner; nor all in the hour of joy, and not all in the hour of retribution; being ready and able to supply one want, and unwilling to supply another. For," as he would add, "does a man want righteousness? there it is laid for him in Christ; does he want merit? there is the treasure full and brimming over; does he want rest and peace? they are also provided for him; does he want faith? there also is faith prepared for him; but the times and the seasons, these are not given to him to know; and, if confusion and every evil work now prevail, Christ being all, he will bring order out of confusion, when the fulness of the time shall come.

"And so," continued the old man, "when it was given me to see and accept this one passage first, in its completeness, all other parts of Scripture seemed to fall at once into their places; and the prophecies; the beautiful prophecies of future peace and joy to the earth, of the destruction of death and of hell, all opened out to me, as being hidden and shut up in

Christ,—for Christ is all; and as I desired the treasure, so I was drawn more and more towards Him who keeps the treasure, and all this," he would add, "was done for me, through no deserts or deservings of my own; for till this light was vouchsafed me, I was as other unregenerate men, living only to myself, and for myself; and more than this," he would say, "were it the Divine will to withdraw the light, I should turn again to be dead and hard, as iron on the cold anvil." In this way, Shanty often used to talk to Mrs. Margaret, and after a while to Tamar; but the old lady for many years remained incapable of entering so entirely as he could wish, into his views of the sufficiency of the Redeemer. She could not give up entirely her notions of the need of some works, not as evidences of the salvation of an individual, but as means of ensuring that salvation, and accordingly she never met with Shanty for many years, without hinting at this discrepancy in their opinions, which hints seldom failed of bringing forward an argument.

When Tamar was about nine years old, Mr. Dymock gave her a dog. Of this creature she was very fond, and always accustomed it to accompany her in her excursions around the Tower. There was on the moor, not many hundred paces from the Tower, a heap of blocks of granite, some of which bore evidence of having been cut with a chisel; but these were almost entirely grown over with saxifrages and other wild plants.

The country people seldom resorted to this place, because they accounted it uncanny, and Mrs. Margaret had several wild tales to tell about it, which greatly interested Tamar. She said, that in the times of papal power, there had been a monastery there, and in that place a covenanter had been murdered; hence, it had been pulled down to the ground, and all the unholy timbers and symbols of idolatry burnt; "and still," she added, "to this day, uncanny objects are seen in that place, and wailings as of souls in woe have also been heard coming from thence; and I myself have heard them. Nay, so short a time ago as the night or two before you, Tamar, were brought a baby to this house, a light was seen there, and unearthly voices heard as coming from thence."

Of course after this, it could not be thought that Tamar should approach this place quite alone, though she often desired to do so; had not Mrs. Margaret told her these stories, she probably might never have had this desire, but there is a principle in human nature, which hankers after the thing forbidden; hence, as St. Paul says, "By the law is the know-ledge of sin." We are not defending human nature, which is indefensible, but merely stating facts. Tamar had much desire to visit this mysterious place; and so it happened one day, when she had her dog with her, and the sun was shining, and all about her bright and gay, that she climbed up the little green knoll, and pushing her way through many brambles, furze bushes, and dwarf shrubs, she found herself in the centre of the huge heaps of stones and rubbish, of which she had hitherto seen only the summits, from the windows of the Tower.

But being arrived there, she came to a stand, to look about her, when her dog, to whom Dymock had given the poetical name of Sappho, began to prick up her ears, and snuff as if she scented something more than ordinary, and the next minute, she dashed forward, made her way through certain bushes, and disappeared. Tamar called aloud; a hollow echo re-sounded her voice, but no dog appeared;—again she called,—again she heard the echo, and again she was silent; but she was by no means a timid child; she had been too much accustomed to be alone,—too much used to explore old corners, of which there were multitudes about the Tower, occupied only by owls and bats. She therefore went forward to the place where Sappho had disappeared, and forcing

Mrs. Sherwood

aside the shrubs, she saw before her a low, arched door-way, which, had she understood architecture, she would have known, from the carvings about the posts and lintel, to have been Norman.

She was surprised, indeed, but thinking only of her dog, she called again, and was perfectly amazed at the long, hollow, and deep sound, of the reverberation. She stood still again, holding the bushes aside, and was aware of a rush of damp vapour, blowing in her face.

Sappho, she called again, and the next minute heard an impatient bark, or yelp, from the animal, and another sound, low, deep and muttering, which she could not comprehend.

She was now getting much alarmed and dropping the boughs, took to flight, and she had scarcely cleared the rubbish, when Sappho came scouring after her, jumping upon her as if glad to see her again. She patted her head, saying "My poor Sappho, what have you seen in that dark place? I wish you had a tongue to tell me."

Tamar immediately returned to the Tower, and hastened to tell her adventure to Mrs. Margaret.

"Oh!" said the old lady, "is it so? that reminds me of what I heard my father say, many and many is the year gone by, that there was an old tradition of a secret passage underground from the Monastery to the Tower; but he never knew where the passage came into the Tower. But be it which way it might, it must needs have passed under the moat."

"How strange!" said Tamar; "but when that passage was made, it could not have been secret; many people must have known it, and I wonder, then, how it could have been so entirely forgotten."

"Who shall say how things were done in those days," said Mrs. Margaret; "those times long past, when things uncanny had more power than they have now? But it is not good to talk of such things," added the lady; "and now, Tamar, let that which you have seen to-day never again be mentioned by you; for, as sure as the master should hear of it, he would be for looking into the cavern, and, Heaven knows what he might stir up, if he were to disturb such things as might be found there. I only wish that that the mischief may not be already done!"

But no mischief did occur, at least for a long time, from this mysterious quarter. Tamar did not again visit the place; and in a short time thought no more of the matter.

The happy days of childhood were passing away with Tamar, and sorrow was coming on her patrons, from a quarter which poor Mrs. Margaret had long darkly anticipated; but whilst these heavy clouds were hanging over the house of Dymock, a few, though not very important events intervened.

Mr. Dymock, by fits and snatches, had given such lessons to Tamar as had enabled her to proceed, by her own exertions, in several branches of knowledge quite out of the sphere of Mrs. Margaret.

Amongst these was the history of the Jews, carried on in connection between the New and Old Testament, and afterwards in Christian times, and to these he added certain crude views of prophecy; for he was resolved that Tamar was a Jewess, and he had talked himself into the belief that she was of some distinguished family.

It is no difficult matter to impress young persons with ideas of their own importance; and none are more liable to receive such impressions, than those who, like Tamar, are in the dark respecting their origin.

The point on which Mr. Dymock failed in his interpretations of prophecy, is not unfrequently mistaken, even in this more enlightened age. He never considered or understood, that all prophecy is delivered in figurative language; every prophecy in the Old Testament having first a literal and incomplete fulfilment, the complete and spiritual fulfilment being future. He did not see that the Jews, according to the flesh, were types of the Spiritual Israel; that David was the emblem of the Saviour; and that the universal kingdom promised to the seed of David, was no other than the kingdom of Christ, into which all the children of God will be gathered together as into one fold under one Shepherd. Not seeing this, he anticipated a period of earthly triumph for the Jews, such as an ambitious, worldly man might anticipate with delight; and he so filled the mind of his young pupil with these notions of the superiority of her race, that it is a miracle that he did not utterly ruin her. As it was, she counted herself greatly superior to all about her, and was much hurt and offended when old Shanty represented the simple truth to her, telling her, that even were she the lineal descendant of Solomon himself, she could have no other privilege than that of the lowest Gentile who has obtained a new birth-right in the Saviour of mankind; "for," said he, "under the Gospel dispensation there is no difference between the Jew and the Greek,—the same Lord over all, is rich unto all that call upon him," Rom. x. 12.

It did not, however, suit Tamar to adopt these truths at the present time; and as Shanty could not succeed with her, he took the liberty of speaking to Mr. Dymock on the subject.

"Why do you fill the young girl's mind, Dymock," said he, "with such fancies as you do? But, leaving her alone, let us speak of the Jews in general. They that wish them well should not fill them up with notions of a birth-right which they have forfeited, and thus confirm them in the very same pride which led them to crucify the Lord of Glory. What is a Jew more than another man? for he is not a Jew which is one outwardly; neither is that circumcision which is outward in the flesh; but he is a Jew which is one inwardly, and circumcision is that of the heart, in the spirit, and not in the letter, whose praise is not of men but of God." Rom. ii. 28, 29.

Mr. Dymock would not listen to honest Shanty on this subject, much as he respected him; and, indeed, the poor Laird was at this time deeply oppressed with other matters.

He had, in his various speculations, so entirely neglected his own affairs for some years past, that poverty, nay actual penury, was staring in his face. He had formerly mortgaged, by little and little, most of his lands, and nothing now remained to make money of, but the Castle itself and a few acres around it, with the exception only of a cottage and a small field, hitherto occupied by a labourer, which lay in a kind of hollow on the side of the knoll, where the entrance of the secret cavern was. This cottage was as remote from Dymock's Tower in one way, as Shanty's shed was in another; although the three dwellings formed together a sort of equilateral triangle. Mr. Dymock long suspected that this labourer had done his share to waste his substance; and once or twice it had occurred to him, that if he left the Castle he might retire to the cottage. But yet, to part with the Castle, could he find a purchaser, would, he feared, be death to Mrs. Margaret, and how would Tamar bear it?—this glorious Maid of Judah, as he was wont to call her,—this palm tree of Zion, this daughter of David,—the very fine person, and very superior air of Tamar having confirmed him in the impression of her noble birth. It was whilst these heavy thoughts respecting what must be done in the management of his affairs dwelt on his mind, that the same man who had finished the unfortunate plough appeared again in Shanty's shed.

The old man recognized him immediately, although fourteen years had much changed his appearance, and he at once charged him with having had some concern with the woman who left the child.

The well-acted astonishment of the vagrant, for such he was, silenced Shanty, though it did not convince him that he was mistaken in his conjecture. However, the old man, changing his mode of attack, and regretting that he had put the stranger on his guard by giving him so home a thrust, pretended to be convinced, and entered into easy conversation with him; amongst other things asking him if perchance he knew of any one who wanted to purchase an estate?

"Aye!" said the vagrant, to whom as we small have the pleasure of introducing him again, we think it may be well to give the name of Harefoot,—"Aye! old gentleman, and might one ask where this estate of yours may be?"

"It is of no consequence," replied Shanty, "I answer no questions, as not being empowered so to do. At all events, however, the estate is not far from hence, and it is a magnificent place, I promise you, More's the pity, that those who have owned it for some hundreds of years, should be compelled to part with it."

Other matters were then introduced, and Shanty endeavoured to wind about Harefoot, but with little success; for, deep as he thought himself, he had one deeper to deal with. In truth, poor Shanty was but a babe in cunning, and the vagrant departed, without having dropped a single hint which could be taken hold of respecting Tamar. In the meantime troubles were pressing upon poor Dymock, the interest of moneys lent on the motgage was not forthcoming, and the Laird having no better friend (and as to a sincerer he needed none,) than poor Shanty, used from day to day to go down to the shed, to open his heart to the old man.

Shanty had long advised his patron to tell his situation to Mrs. Margaret, and to advertise the sale of the castle, but Dymock's pride had not yet so far submitted itself, as to enable him to make so public a confession of the downfall of the family, as an advertisement would do.

"I cannot open my heart to my aunt, Shanty," he said, "she, poor creature, has devoted her whole life to keeping up the dignity of the house; how, then, will she bear to see the whole labour of her life annihilated?"

"The sooner she knows of what is coming the better," returned Shanty, "if she is not prepared, the blow when it comes, will go nigh utterly to overpower her," and the old man proposed to go himself, to open the matter to her.

"You shall, Shanty, you shall," said the Laird, "but wait a little, wait a little, we may hear of a purchaser for the castle, and when such a one is found, then you shall speak to my aunt."

"But first," said Shanty, "let me prepare your adopted one, let me open the matter to her; she is of an age, in which she ought to think and act no longer as a child; it is now fourteen years since I carried her up in my arms to Dymock's Tower, and though the young girl is too much filled up with pride, yet I fear not but that she is a jewel, which will shine brighter, when rubbed under the wheel of adversity; allowing what I hope, that there is a jewel under that crust of pride."

Mrs. Sherwood

"Pride!" repeated Dymock, flying off into the region of romance, "and if a daughter of Zion, a shoot from the Cedar of Lebanon, is not to carry her head high, who is to do so? the fate of her race may indeed follow her, and she may be brought down, to sit in the dust, but still even in the dust, she may yet boast her glorious origin."

Shanty raised his hands and eyes, "Lord help you! Dymock," he said, "but you are clean demented. I verily believe, that the child is nothing mere than the offspring of a begging gipsy, and that if her mother had been hanged, she would only have met with her deserts."

Discussions of this kind were constantly taking place between Shanty and Dymock, and it was in the very midst of one these arguments, that the rare appearance of a hired chaise,—a job and pair, as Shanty called it, appeared coming over the moor, directly to the shed, and so quick was the approach, that the Laird and the blacksmith had by no means finished their conjectures respecting this phenomenon, before the equipage came to a stand, in the front of the hut.

As the carriage stopped, a spare, sallow, severe looking old gentlemen, put his head out of the window, and calling to the post boy, in a sharp, querulous tone, asked if he were quite sure that he was right?

"Not sure that this is old Shanty's hut; Shanty of Dymock's Moor," replied the post-boy, in a broad Northern accent; "ask me if I don't know my own mother's son, though she never had but one bairn."

Dymock and Shanty no sooner heard the voice of the boy, than they both recognized him, and stepping forward, they went up to the carriage and offered to assist the old gentleman to alight; he received their civilities with very little courtesy. However, he got out of the carriage, and giving himself a shake, and a sort of twist, which caused the lappets of his coat to expand, like the fan-tail of a pigeon, he asked, if the place was Dymock's Moor, and if the old man he saw before him, was one called Shanty of the Moor? The blacksmith declared himself to be that same person, "and this gentlemen," he added, pointing to Dymock, whose every day dress, by the bye, did not savor much of the Laird, "This gentleman is Dymock himself."

"Ah, is it so," said the stranger, "my business then is with him, show me where I can converse with him."

"I have no parlour to offer you," said Shanty; "to my shed, however, such as it is, I make you welcome."

No gracious notice was taken by the stranger of the offer, but without preamble or ceremony, he told his errand to Mr. Dymock. "I hear," he said, "that you wish to sell your Tower, and the lands which surround it; if after looking at it, and finding that it suits me, you will agree to let me have it, I will pay you down in moneys, to the just and due amount of the value thereof, but first I must see it."

"It stands there, Sir," said Shanty, seeing that Mr. Dymock's heart was too full to permit him to speak; "it stands there, Sir, and is as noble an object as my eye ever fell upon. The Tower," continued the old man, "at this minute, lies directly under the only dark cloud now in the heavens; nevertheless, a slanting ray from the westering sun now falls on its highest turret; look on, Sir, and say wherever have you seen a grander object?"

The old gentleman uttered an impatient pish, and said, "Old man, your travels must needs have lain in small compass, if you think much of yon heap of stones and rubbish." The

Mrs. Sherwood

Laird's choler was rising, and he would infallibly have told the stranger to have walked himself off, if Shanty had not pulled him by the sleeve, and, stepping before the stranger, said something in a soothing way, which should enhance the dignity of the Tower and encourage the pretended purchaser.

"I must see it, I must see it," returned the old gentleman, "not as now mixed up with the clouds, but I must examine it, see its capabilities, and know precisely what it is worth, and how it can be secured to me and my heirs for ever."

It was warm work which poor Shanty now had to do; between the irritated seller and the testy buyer, he had never been in a hotter place before his own forge, and there was wind enough stirring in all reason, without help of bellows, for the Laird puffed and groaned and uttered half sentences, and wished himself dead, on one side of the old blacksmith, whilst the stranger went on as calmly, coolly, and deliberately, with his bargain, on the other side, as if he were dealing with creatures utterly without feeling. Shanty turned first to one, and then to another; nodding and winking to Dymock to keep quiet on one side, whilst he continued to vaunt the merits of the purchase on the other.

At length, on a somewhat more than usually testy remark of the stranger reaching the ears of the Laird, he burst by Shanty and had already uttered these words, "Let me hear no more of this, I am a gentleman, and abominate the paltry consideration of pounds, shillings, and pence;" when Shanty forcibly seizing his arm, turned him fairly round, whispering, "Go, and for the sake of common sense, hold your tongue, leave the matter to me, let me bargain for you; go and tell Mrs. Margaret that we are coming, and make what tale you will to her, to explain our unceremonious visit; you had better have told her all before."

The Laird informed Shanty that there was no need of going up to the Tower to inform his aunt, as she and Tamar were gone that day over the border to visit a friend; but added he, "I take your offer, Shanty, make the bargain for me if you can, and I shall not appear till I am wanted to sign and seal," and away marched the Laird nor was he forthcoming again for some hours.

After he was gone, Shanty begged leave to have a few minutes given him for washing his hands and face and making himself decent, and then walked up with the testy old gentlemen to the castle. Little as Shanty knew of the great and grand world, yet his heart misgave him, lest the ruinous state of the castle, (although the Tower itself stood in its ancient and undilapidated strength,) should so entirely disgust the stranger that he should at once renounce all ideas of the purchase; he was therefore much pleased when the old gentleman, having gone grumbling and muttering into every room and every outhouse, crying, it is naught! it is naught! as buyers generally do, bade Shanty tell the Laird that he was going to the nearest town, that he should be there till the business was settled, that he would give the fair valuation for the estate, and that the payment should be prompt.

Shanty was, indeed astonished; he was all amazement, nor did he recover himself, till he saw the old gentleman walk away, and get into his carriage which was waiting on the other side of the moat, it not being particularly convenient, on account of the total deficiency of anything like a bridge or passable road? to bring a carriage larger than a wheel-barrow up to the castle.

Dymock returned to the shed, when he, from some place of observation on the moor, saw that the carriage had reached the high road, and there, having been told all that had passed, the poor gentleman (who, by the bye, was not half pleased

Mrs. Sherwood

with the idea of the honours of Dymock falling into the hands of such a purchaser,) informed Shanty that he must prepare to go with him the next day to Hexham, where the stranger had appointed to meet him.

"I go with you!" exclaimed Shanty, "was ever so strange a conceit."

"I shall be fleeced, shorn, ruined," implied Mr. Dymock, "if I go to make a bargain, without a grain of common sense in my company."

"True," returned Shanty, "your worship is right; but how are we to go? I have plenty of horse-shoes by me, but neither you, nor I Laird, I fear could find any four legs to wear them."

"We must e'en walk then," said Dymock, "nay, I would gladly carry you on my back, rather than descend to the meanness of driving a bargain with a testy old fellow like that; by the bye, Shanty, what does he call himself?"

"Salmon," replied Shanty, "and I mistake if he has not a touch of the foreigner on his tongue."

"You will accompany me, then Shanty," said the Laird.

"I will," he replied, "if this evening you will open the business out to Mrs. Margaret."

"It cannot be Shanty," replied Dymock chuckling, "for she does not expect to be back over the border till to-morrow, and when to-morrow is over and we know what we are about, then you shall tell her all."

"Dymock," said Shanty, "you are hard upon me, when you

have a morsel to swallow that is too tough for you, you put it into my mouth; but," added the old man kindly, "there is not much that I would refuse to do for your father's son."

The sun had not yet risen over the moor, when Dymock and Shanty, both arrayed in their best, set off for Hexham, where they found the crabbed old gentlemen, still in the humour of making the purchase, though he abused the place in language at once rude and petulant; his offer, however, was, as Shanty compelled Dymock to see, a very fair one, though the more sensible and wary blacksmith could not persuade his friend to beware of trusting anything to the honour of Mr. Salmon.

Dymock's estate had been deeply mortgaged, the sale was made subject to the mortgages, and the purchaser was bound to pay the mortgagee the mortgage moneys, after which there was small surplus coming to poor Dymock. This small surplus was, however, paid down on the signing of the papers; still, however, there was an additional payment to take place soon after possession.

This payment was, it was supposed, to be for fixtures and other articles, which were to be left on the premises, and it was not to be asked till Mr. Salmon had been resident a few weeks. The amount was between five and six hundred pounds, and was in fact all that Dymock would have to depend upon besides his cottage, his field, a right of shooting on the moor, and fishing in a lake which belonged to the estate, and about twenty pounds a year which appertained to Mrs. Margaret, from which it was supposed she had made some savings.

Shanty had succeeded in forcing the Laird to listen to the dictates of prudence, and to act with sufficient caution, till it came to what he called the dirty part of the work, to wit, the valuation of small articles, and then was the blood of the

Dymocks all up; nor would he hear of requiring a bond for the payment of this last sum, such a document, in fact, as should bind the purchaser down to payment without dispute. He contented himself only with such a note from the old man as ought he asserted to be quite sufficient, and it was utterly useless for Shanty to expostulate. The Laird had got on his high horse and was prancing and capering beyond all the controul of his honest friend, whilst Mr. Salmon, no doubt, laughed in his sleeve, and only lamented that he had not known Dymock better from the first, for in that case he would have used his cunning to have obtained a better bargain of the castle and lands. It was not one nor two visits to Hexham which completed these arrangements; however Mr. Dymock, after the first visit, no longer refused to permit Shanty to open out every thing to his aunt, and to prepare her to descend into a cottage, on an income of forty or fifty pounds a year.

Mrs. Margaret bore the information better than Shanty had expected; she had long anticipated some such blow, and her piety enabled her to bear it with cheerfulness. "I now," she said, "know the worst, and I see not wherefore, though I am a Dymock, I should not be happy in a cottage, I am only sorry for Tamar; poor Tamar! what will become of her?"

"Oh mother! dear mother!" said Tamar weeping, "why are you sorry for me, cannot I go with you? surely you would not part from me;" and she fell weeping on Mrs. Margaret's bosom.

"Never before! oh, never before," cried Mrs. Margaret, "did I feel my poverty as I do now."

"Mother dear! oh mother dear! had I thousands of pounds, I would devote them all to you, and to my dear protector."

"God helping you, or God working in you Tamar," said Shanty, rubbing his rough hand across his eyes, "but never boast of what you will do, dear child; boasting does not suit the condition of humanity."

"Oh! that I could now find my father," she replied, "and if I could find him a rich man, what a comfort it would be; what would I give now," she added, "to find a rich father!"

Mrs. Margaret kissed her child, and wept with her, calling her a dear, affectionate, grateful creature; but Shanty made no remark respecting Tamar's gratitude; he had it in his mind to speak to her when alone, and he very soon found the opportunity he wished.

It was on the next Sunday that he met Tamar walking on the moor, and it was then that he thus addressed her, "I was sorry damsel," he said, "to hear you speak as you did to Mrs. Margaret the other day, making a profession of what you would do for her if you were rich, and yet never offering her that which you have to give her."

"What have I to give her?" asked Tamar.

"Much," replied the old man; "much, very much. You have strength, and activity, and affection to give her. With forty pounds a-year, a house, and a little field, which is all your adopted parents will have, can they, think you, keep a servant? Will not the very closest care be necessary, and should not one who is young, and faithful, and attached, rejoice to serve her benefactors at such time as this, and to render their fall as easy as possible; and where, I ask you, Tamar, should they find such service as you can render them?"

They were walking side by side, the old man and the

beautiful girl, among the heather of the moor; and he was looking up kindly and animatedly to her,—for he was a remarkably short, thick-set man,—but she was looking down on the ground, whilst a bitter struggle was passing in her mind. She had been filled up by her guardian with wild fancies of her own greatness, which was hereafter to be made manifest; and it would have been too strong for unaided nature, to bring herself to submit to such drudgeries as duty seemed now to require of her; her bright-brown cheek was flushed with the inward contest, and her bosom seemed to be almost swelled to suffocation. But the assistance required was not withheld in the hour of need, and Shanty was soon made aware of the change of feelings which was suddenly imparted to the orphan by the change of the expression of her countenance; the tears had already filled her eyes, when she turned to her old friend, and thanked him for his reproof, expressing her conviction, that his advice was that of a true Christian, and begging him always to tell her, in like manner, when he saw that she was going wrong. A more general discussion on the subject of true religion then followed, and Shanty assured Tamar, that all high notions of self, whether of birth, talents, or riches, were unpleasing in the sight of God, and utterly inconsistent with that view of salvation by Christ, which is independent of all human merit. Such was the nature of the lessons given by the old man to Tamar. His language was, however, broad, and full of north-country phrases, so much so, as to have rendered them inexplicable to one who had not been accustomed to the Border dialect. From that day, however, through the divine mercy, the heart of Tamar was given to the duties which she saw before her, and all her activity was presently put into requisition; for Mr. Salmon had given notice, that he should take possession of Dymock's Tower as soon as it could be got ready for him, and he also sent persons to make the preparations which he required. These preparations were of a most singular nature; his object appeared neither to be the beautifying of the old place, or even the rendering it more comfortable, for he neither sent new furniture, nor ordered the restoration of any of the dilapidated chambers or courts. But he ordered the moat to be repaired, so that it could be filled and kept full, and he directed that a light draw-bridge should also be erected. The walls of the inner courts were also to be put to rights, and new gates added. There was a great laugh in the country respecting this unknown humourist; and some said he was preparing for a siege, and others going to set up for a modern Rob Roy, and Castle-Dymock was to be his head-quarters.

The greater part of the furniture, and all the fixtures, were to be paid for by the money for which the Laird had Mr. Salmon's memorandum; and they who knew their condition, said that the things had been brought to a good market, as little of the furniture would have been worth the carriage across the moor. Nothing at present, therefore, remained for the aunt and the nephew to do, but to remove to the cottage as soon as it should be ready to receive them.

This humble habitation was situated in a small nook or vale of the moor called Heatherdale. A little fresh-water spring ran through it, coming in at the higher end of the valley, and going out through a natural cleft in a block of granite at the other end. There were many tall trees scattered on the banks within the dell; and the place was so sheltered, that many a plant would flourish in the garden on the south side of the house, which could hardly be kept alive in any other situation in the country.

The cottage was an old, black, timbered and thatched edifice, and had four rooms of considerable dimensions, two above and two below, with a porch in the front, overgrown with briony and another hardy creeper. As soon as this tenement was vacated, and the Laird's intention of inhabiting it known,

Mrs. Sherwood

the ancient tenants of the family all manifested their affection by using their several crafts in repairing the cottage, and setting the house to rights,—one mended the thatch, another repaired the wood-work, a third white-washed the walls, another mended the paling, and old Shanty did any little job in his way which might be required.

The labours of love never hang long on hand, and though the old tenant had gone out only at Lady-day, the hawthorn had scarcely blossomed when the affectionate people pronounced the work complete.

Poor Dymock had become very restless when he saw the changes which were going on at the Tower; but when there was no longer an excuse to be found for delaying the removal, he gave way altogether, or rather, we should say, made a cut and run, and went off to botanize the lakes in Westmoreland, with a knapsack on his back, and a guinea in his pocket.

Before he went, however, he had opened his heart to his daughter Tamar, saying, "I now take leave, dear child, of the life of a gentleman; henceforward I must content myself with the corner of a kitchen ingle; and this, truly, is a berth," he added, "too good for a cumberer of the ground, such as I am." He said this as he passed through the gate of the court, giving his adopted one time only to snatch his hand and kiss it, and he was gone beyond her hearing before she could relieve her heart with a burst of tears. After a while, however, she dried them up, and began to busy her mind in thinking what she could do to render the cottage comfortable for her beloved guardian; and having at length formed her plan, she ran to Mrs. Margaret, and asked her permission to take the arrangement of their new house.

"Let me," said she, "see all the things put in their places; you and I, dear aunt Margaret, will have to ourselves a kitchen as neat as a palace, and we will make a study of the inner room for Mr. Dymock."

"What!" said the old lady, "and give up our parlour?"

"Dear mother," replied the young girl carelessly, "if there is to be no maid but poor Tamar, why should not the kitchen be the happiest place, for her own dear mother? You shall have your chair in the corner, between the window and the fire-place, and your little work-table by it, and then you can direct me without moving from your needle. Oh! dear, aunt Margaret," she added, "I am beginning to think that we shall be happier in the cottage, than we have been in the Castle; we shall have fewer cares, and shall have a pleasure in putting our small means to the best. Do not the scatterings of the flock, aunt Margaret, make us as warm hose as the prime of the fleece?"

"That may be doubted child," replied the old lady with a smile, "but go young creature, take your way; I believe ere yet you have done, that you, with your sunny smile, will cheat me into contentment before I know what I am about; but mind, my lovely one," she added, "I will tell you how it is. I have been led to see how God in his displeasure,—displeasure, I say, on account of the pride of ancestry and station, which I have hitherto persisted in cherishing,—how God, I repeat, in his displeasure has remembered mercy, and, in taking away that which is worthless, has left me that which is most precious, even you my bright one."

The old lady then kissed Tamar, and gave her the permission she required, to arrange the cottage according to her own fancy. When the day of removal actually arrived, being the day after the Laird had walked himself off, the neighbours, with Shanty at their head, came to assist.

Tamar had determined upon having the room within the kitchen, for her beloved father by adoption; a village artist having understood her pious wish, had stained the walls of light grey, and painted the frame of the casement window of the same colour. Tamar had prepared a curtain of some light drapery for the window; a well-darned carpet covered the floor, the Laird's bookcases occupied one entire end of the room opposite the window, the wonted table of the old study at the Tower was placed in the centre of the floor, and was covered with its usual cloth, a somewhat tarnished baize, with a border worked in crewels by Mrs. Margaret in days gone by. In the centre of this table the inkstand was placed, and on the opposite wall, a venerable time-piece, asserted, with what truth we presume not to say, to be nearly as old as the clock sent by Haroun Al Raschid to the emperor Charlemagne. A few high-backed chairs, certain strange chimney ornaments, and other little matters dear to the Laird, finished the furniture of this room, and Tamar perfectly laughed with joy, when, having seen all done, she became aware that this small apartment was in fact more comfortable than the cold, wide, many-drafted study in the Tower.

Those who were with her caught the merry infection and laughed too, and Shanty said, "But dear one, whilst you thus rejoice in your own contrivances, have you not a word of praise to give to Him, who has spread such glories as no human skill could create, beyond yon little window?" The old man then opened the casement, and showed the sweet and peaceful scene which there presented itself; for the cottage was enclosed in a small dell, the green sides of which seemed to shut out all the world, enclosing within their narrow limits, a running brook, and hives of bees, and many fragrant flowers.

Tamar was equally successful, and equally well pleased with her arrangements in other parts of the cottage; the kitchen opened on one side to a little flower garden, on the other to the small yard, where Mrs. Margaret intended to keep her poultry, and the whole domain was encompassed by the small green field, which made up the extent of the dell, and was the only bit of land left to the representative of the house of Dymock. But Mrs. Margaret had reckoned that the land would keep a little favourite cow, and with this object Tamar had taken great pains to learn to milk.

When all was ready, Mrs. Margaret with many tears took leave of Dymock's Tower; she had not seen the process of preparation in the cottage, and was therefore perfectly astonished when she entered the house. Tamar received her with tears of tenderness, and the worthy lady having examined all the arrangements, blessed her adopted one, and confessed that they had all in that place that man really required. Neither did she or Tamar find that they had more to do than was agreeable; if they had no servants to wait upon them, they had no servants to disarrange their house. They had engaged an old cottager on the moor to give them an hour's work every evening, and for this they paid him with a stoup of milk, or some other small product of their dairy; money they had not to spare, and this he knew,—nor did he require any; he would have given his aid to the fallen family for nothing, had it been asked of him.

In wild and thinly peopled countries, there is more of neigh-bourly affection,—more of private kindness and sympathy than in crowded cities. Man is a finite creature; he cannot take into his heart many objects at once, and such, indeed, is the narrowness of his comprehension, that he cannot even conceive how the love of an infinite being can be generally exercised through creation. It is from this incapacity that religious people, at least too many of them, labour so sedulously as they do to instil the notion of the particularity of the work of salvation, making it almost to appear, that the

Mrs. Sherwood

Almighty Father brings beings into existence, merely to make them miserable,—but we are wandering from our story.

Aunt Margaret and Tamar had been at the cottage a fortnight before Dymock returned; Tamar saw him first coming down the glen, looking wearied, dispirited and shabby.

She ran out to meet her adopted father, and sprang into his arms; his eyes were filled with tears, and her bright smiles caused those eyes to overflow.

She took his hand, she brought him in, she set him a chair, and Mrs. Margaret kissing him, said "Come Dymock brighten up, and thank your God for a happy home."

Dymock sighed, Tamar took his heavy knapsack from him, and placed before him bread and butter, and cheese, and a stoup of excellent beer.

"Eat, dear father," she said, "and then you shall go to bed, (for it was late in the evening,) and to-morrow you will see what a sweet place this is;" but poor Dymock could not rally that night. Tamar had always slept with Mrs. Margaret, and the best room of the two above stairs had been prepared for Dymock, Mrs. Margaret having found a place under the rafters for her innumerable boxes.

The poor Laird slept well, and when he awoke the sun was shining into his room, and aunt Margaret had arranged his clean clothes at the foot of his bed; he arose in better spirits, and dressing himself, he went down; he found Tamar in the kitchen, and she, without speaking, took his hand and led him to his study.

The poor gentleman could not bear this: he saw the sacrifice his aunt had made for him, and the exertions also which Tamar must have made to produce this result, and he fairly wept; but this burst of agitation being over, he embraced his adopted child, and expressed his earnest hope that henceforward he might be enabled to live more closely with his God.

But the mind of Dymock was not a well balanced one; he could not live without a scheme, and he had scarcely been two days in the cottage, when he re-aimed at the ideas which he had formerly indulged of becoming an author, and of obtaining both fame and money by his writings. Mrs. Margaret was fretted when she was made aware of this plan, and sent Tamar to Shanty, to ask him to talk him out of the fancy, and to persuade him to adopt some employment, if it were only digging in his garden, which might bring in something; but Shanty sent Tamar back to Mrs. Margaret to tell her that she ought to be thankful that there was anything found which would keep the Laird easy and quiet, and out of the way of spending the little which he had left. Poor Dymock, therefore, was not disturbed in his attempts at authorship, and there he used to sit in his study with slip-shod feet, an embroidered dressing gown, which Mrs. Margaret had quilted from an old curtain, and a sort of turban twisted about his head, paying no manner of attention to hours or seasons. As Mrs. Margaret only allowed him certain inches of candle, he could not sit up all night as geniuses ought to be permitted to do; but then he would arise with the lark and set to work, before any of the labourers on the moor were in motion. In vain did Mrs. Margaret complain and expostulate; she even in her trouble sent Tamar again to Shanty to request him to plead with the Laird, and beg him to allow himself to enjoy his regular rest; but in this case when she required Shanty's aid, she had reckoned without her host.

Mrs. Sherwood

"Go back to Mrs. Margaret, damsel," he said, "go and tell the lady that as long as she can keep the Laird from work by candle light, so long no harm is done, and if instead of murmuring at this early rising, fair child, you will take example by him, and leave your bed at the same time that your hear him go down, you will do well. He that lies in bed gives a daily opportunity to his servants, if he has any to serve him, to do mischief before he is up, and she that rises with the sun and goes straight forward, like an arrow in its course, in the path of her duties, shall find fewer thorns and more roses in that path, than those who indulge in ease. Through divine mercy," continued the old man, "our own exertions are not needed for the assurance of our salvation, but sloth and carelessness tend to penury and misery, in this present life; and there is no sloth more ruinous to health and property than that of wasting the precious morning hours in bed."

Tamar was not deaf to the pleadings of Shanty; she began immediately to rise with the first crowing of the cock, and thus obtained so much time for her business, that she could then afford herself some for reading. Mrs. Margaret took also to rise early, so that instead of breakfasting as formerly at eight o'clock, the family took that meal at seven; but the Laird often managed to have such bright and valuable thoughts just at breakfast time, that for the sake of posterity, as he was wont to say, he could by no means endanger the loss of them by suffering such a common place interruption as that of breakfast, such an every day and vulgar concern. On these occasions Tamar always took in his coffee and toast, and set it before him, and she generally had the pleasure of finding that he took what she brought him, though he seldom appeared to be aware either of her entrance or her exit, Mrs. Margaret invariably exclaiming when Tamar reported her reception in the study, "Lord help him! see what it is to be a genius!"

In the meantime, the moat around Dymock's Tower was repaired and filled up, or was fast filling up; the draw-bridge was in its place, and the gates and walls restored; and as the neighbours said, the Tower wanted nothing but men and provisions to enable it to stand a siege. At length, all being pronounced ready, though no interior repairing had taken place, the new possessor arrived, bringing with him two servants, an old man and an old woman, and many heavy packages, which were stowed in a cart, and lifted out by himself and his man-servant, whom he called Jacob. This being done, he and his people were heard of no more, or rather seen no more, being such close housekeepers, that they admitted no one over the moat, though the man Jacob, rode to the nearest market every week on the horse which had dragged the baggage, to bring what was required, which, it was said, was not much more than was necessary to keep the bodies and souls of three people together.

Numerous and strange were the speculations made by all people on the moor upon these new tenants of Dymock's Tower, and Shanty's shed was a principal scene of these speculations. Various were the reproaches which were cast on the strangers, and no name was too bad for them.

"Our old Laird," one remarked, "was worth ten thousand such. As long as he had a crust, he would divide it with any one that wanted it. Mark but his behaviour to the poor orphan, who is now become the finest girl, notwithstanding her dark skin, in all the country round."

Then followed speculations on the parentage of Tamar, and old Shanty asserted that he believed her to be nothing more or less than the daughter of the gipsy hag who had laid her at his door. Some said she was much to good to be the child of a gipsy; and then Shanty asserted, that the grace of God could counteract not only the nature of a child of a vagrant of the worst description, but even that of such vagrant himself; the Spirit of God being quick and powerful, and sharper than a two-edged sword.

Shanty was a sort of oracle amongst his simple neighbours, and what he said was not often disputed to his face; nevertheless, there was not an individual on the moor who knew Tamar, who did not believe her to be a princess in disguise or something very wonderful; and, at the bottom of her heart, poor Tamar still indulged this same belief, though she did not now, as formerly express it.

It was in the month of June, very soon after, Mr. Salmon had arrived at the Tower, and before Dymock, who was a woful procrastinator, had gone to demand the last payment, that Tamar, who was extraordinarily light and active, had undertaken to walk to the next village to procure some necessaries; she had three miles to go over the moor, nor could she go till after dinner. Her way lay by Shanty's shed; and Mrs. Margaret admonished her, if anything detained her, to call on Shanty, and ask him to walk over the remainder of the moor with her on her return.

When she came down from preparing herself for this walk, all gay and blooming with youth and health, and having a basket on her arm, she met Dymock in the little garden.

"Whither away? beautiful Maid of Judah," said the genius. "My bright-eyed Tamar," he added, "I have been thinking of a poem, and if I can but express my ideas, it will be the means of lifting up my family again from the destitution into which it has fallen. My subject is the restoration of Jerusalem in the latter days, and the lifting up of the daughters of Zion from the dust. The captives of Israel now are hewers of wood and carriers of water; but the time will come when the hands that now wear the manacles of servitude shall be comely with rows of jewels."

"If no daughter of Judah," replied Tamar, "wears heavier manacles than I do, dear father, they may bear them with light hearts;" and, as she passed quickly by her adopted father, she snatched his hand and kissed it, and soon she disappeared beyond the boundary of the glen.

Tamar reached the village in so short a time, and did her errands so quickly, that having some hours of light before her, she thought she would try another way of return, over a small bridge, which in fact spanned the very water-course which ran through her glen; but being arrived at this bridge, to her surprise she found it broken down. It was only a single plank, and the wood had rotted and given way. The brook was too wide and deep in that place to permit her to cross it, and the consequence was, that she must needs go round more than a mile; and, what added to her embarrassment, the evening, which had been fine, was beginning to cloud over, the darkness of the sky hastening the approach of the dusk. She had now farther to walk than she had when in the village; and, added to the threatenings of the clouds, there were frequent flashings of pale lightning, and remote murmurings of thunder. But Tamar was not easily alarmed; she had been brought up independently, and already had she recovered the direct path from the village to Shanty's shed, when suddenly a tall figure of a female arose, as it were, out of the broom and gorse, and stepped in the direction in which she was going, walking by her side for a few paces without speaking a word.

The figure was that of a gipsy, and the garments, as Tamar glanced fearfully at them as they floated in a line with her steps, bespoke a variety of wretchedness scarcely consistent with the proud and elastic march of her who wore them.

Whilst Tamar felt a vague sense of terror stealing over her, the woman spoke, addressing her without ceremony, saying, "So you have been driven to come this way at last; have you been so daintily reared that you cannot wade a burn which has scarcely depth enough to cover the pebbles in its channel. Look you," she added, raising her arm, and pointing her finger,—"see you yon rising ground to the left of those fir trees on the edge of the moor,—from the summit of that height the sea is visible, and I must, ere many hours, be upon those waters, in such a bark as you delicately-bred dames would not confide in on a summer's day on Ulswater Mere."

Whilst the woman spoke, Tamar looked to her and then from her, but not a word did she utter.

"Do you mind me?" said the gipsy; "I have known you long, aye very long. You were very small when I brought you to this place. I did well for you then. Are you grateful?"

Tamar now did turn and look at her, and looked eagerly, and carefully, and intently on her dark and weather-beaten countenance.

"Ah!" said the gipsy, whilst a smile of scorn distorted her lip,—"so you will demean yourself now to look upon me; and you would like to know what I could tell you?"

"Indeed, indeed, I would!" exclaimed Tamar, all flushed and trembling. "Oh, in pity, in mercy tell me who I am and who are my parents?—if they still live; if I have any chance or—hope of seeing them?"

"One is no more," replied the gipsy. "She from whom I took you lies in the earth on Norwood Common. I stretched the corpse myself,—it was a bonny corpse."

Tamar fetched a deep, a very deep sigh. "Does my father live?" she asked.

"Your father!" repeated the gipsy, with a malignant laugh,—"your father!"

Tamar became more and more agitated; but excessive feeling made her appear almost insensible. With great effort she repeated,—"Does my father live?"

"He does," replied the woman, with a malignant smile, "and shall I tell you where and how?—shut up, confined in a strong-hold, caught like a vile animal in a trap. Do you understand me, Tamar? I think they call you Tamar."

"What!" said the poor girl, gasping for breath, "is my father a convicted felon?"

"I used no such words," replied the gipsy; "but I told you that he lies shut up; and he is watched and guarded, too, I tell you."

"Then he has forfeited his liberty," said Tamar; "he has committed some dreadful crime. Tell me, Oh! tell me, what is it?"

The gipsy laughed, and her laugh was a frightful one.

"What!" she said, "are you disappointed?—is the blight come over you? has the black fog shut out all the bright visions which the foolish Laird created in your fancy? Go, child!" she said, "go and tell him what I have told you, and see whether he will continue to cherish and flatter the offspring of our vagrant race."

"He will," replied Tamar; "but tell me, only tell me, what is that mark burnt upon my shoulder?"

"Your father branded you," she answered, "as we do all our children, lest in our many wanderings we should lose sight of our own, and not know them again; but come," she added, "the night draws on, darkness is stealing over the welkin; you are for the shed; there is your pole-star; see you the fitful glare of the forge?—I am for another direction; fare-you-well."

"Stay, stay," said Tamar, seizing her arm, "Oh, tell me more! tell me more! My father, if I have a living father, I owe him a duty,—where is he? Tell me where he is, for the love of heaven tell me?"

The woman shook her off,—"Go, fool," she said, "you know enough; or stay," she added, in her turn seizing Tamar's arm,—"if you like it better, leave those Dymocks and come with me, and you shall be one with us, and live with us, and eat with us and drink with us."

"No! no!" said Tamar, with a piercing shriek, disengaging herself from the gipsy, and running with the swiftness of a hare, towards the friendly hovel.

Old Shanty was alone, when, all pale and trembling, Tamar entered the shed, and sunk, half fainting, on the very bench on which the gipsy had sate on the eventful night in which she had brought her to the hovel fourteen years before.

Shanty was terrified, for he had a paternal feeling for Tamar; he ceased immediately from his hammering, and sitting himself by her on the bench, he rested not until she had told him every thing which had happened; and when she had done so,—"Tamar," he said, "I am not surprised; I never thought you any thing else than the child of a vagrant, nor had you ever any ground for thinking otherwise. There are many imaginations," added the pious old man, "which attend our nature, which must be destroyed before we can enter into that perfect union with the Son, which will render us one with the Father, and will insure our happiness when God shall be all in all, and when all that is foretold in prophecy respecting this present earth shall be completed. Sin," continued the old man, "is neither more nor less than the non-conformity of the will of the creature with that of the Creator; and when the will of every child of Adam is brought into unison with the divine pleasure, then, as far our race is concerned, there will be an end of sin; and, in particular cases, Tamar, as regarding individuals in the present and past days, each one is happy, not as far as he indulges the imaginations suggested by his own depraved nature, but as far as he is content to be what his God would have him to be, as indicated by the circumstances and arrangements of things about him."

It was marvellous (or rather would have been so to a stranger,) to hear this poor old dusky blacksmith, speaking and reasoning as he did; but who shall limit or set bounds to the power of the Lord the Spirit in enlightening the mind, independently as it were, of human ministry, or at least of any other ministry than that which teaches and promulgates the mere letter of Scripture?

Tamar's mind was at that time fully prepared to receive all that Shanty said to her, and, insensibly to themselves, they were presently led almost to forget the information given by the gipsy, (which in fact left Tamar just as it had found her,) whilst new thoughts were opening to them; and the young girl was brought to see, that in her late anxiety to render the kind friends who had adopted her, comfortable as to outward circumstances, she had failed in using her filial influence to draw their attention to thoughts of religion.

Mrs. Sherwood

Shanty put on his coat, and walked with her over the rest of the moor, nor did he leave Heatherdale (where Mrs. Margaret insisted that he should sup,) until he had opened out to the Laird and his aunt the whole history of Tamar's rencounter with the gipsy. It was curious to observe the effect of this story on the minds of the two auditors. Mrs. Margaret embraced Tamar with tears, saying, "Methinks I am rejoiced that there is no one likely to claim my precious one from me;" whilst the Laird exclaimed, "I am not in the least convinced. The gipsy has no doubt some scheme of her own in view. She is afraid of being found out, and transported for child-stealing; but I wish I could see her, to tell her that I no more believe my palm-tree to have sprung from the briers of the Egyptian wilderness, than that I am not at this moment the Laird of Dymock."

"Lord help you, nephew!" said Mrs. Margaret, "if poor dear Tamar's noble birth has not more substantial foundation than your lairdship, I believe that she must be content as she is,— the adopted daughter of a poor spinster, who has nothing to leave behind her but a few bales of old clothes."

"Contented, my mother," said Tamar, bursting into tears, "could I be contented if taken from you?"

Thus the affair of the gipsy passed off. The Laird, indeed, talked of raising the country to catch the randy quean; but all these resolutions were speedily forgotten, and no result ensued from this alarm, but that which Almighty power produced from it in the mind of Tamar, by making her more anxious to draw the minds of her patrons to religion.

After this, for several weeks things went on much as usual on Dymock's moor. The inhabitants of the Tower were so still and quiet, that unless a thin curl of smoke had now and then been seen rising from the kitchen chimney, all the occupants might have been supposed to have been in a state of enchantment. Jacob, however, the dwarfish, deformed serving-man, did cross the moat at intervals, and came back laden with food; but he was so surly and short, that it was impossible to get a word of information from him, respecting that which was going on within the moat. Whilst Dymock scribbled, his aunt darned, Shanty hammered, and Tamar formed the delight and comfort of all the three last mentioned elders. But some settlement was necessarily to be made respecting Mr. Salmon's last payment, which had run up, with certain fixtures and old pictures, for which there was no room in the cottage, to nearly six hundred pounds, and after much pressing and persuading on the part of Mrs. Margaret, the Laird was at length worked up to the point of putting on his very best clothes, and going one morning to the Tower. He had boasted that he would not appear but as the Laird of Dymock in Dymock castle; therefore, though the weather was warm, he assumed his only remains of handsome apparel, viz, a cloak or mantle of blue cloth and with a hat, which was none of the best shape, on his head, he walked to the edge of the moat, and there stood awhile calling aloud.

At length Jacob appeared on the other side, and knowing the Laird, he turned the bridge, over which Dymock walked with sullen pride.

"I would see your master, where is he?" said the Laird, as soon as he got into the court.

The eye of the dwarf directed that of Dymock to the window of a small room in a higher part of the keep, and the Laird, without waiting further permission, walked forward into the Tower.

It gave him pain to see all the old and well remembered

Mrs. Sherwood

objects again; but it also gave him pleasure to find every-thing in its place as he had left it—even the very dust on the mouldings and cornices, which had remained undisturbed through the reign of Mrs. Margaret, from the absolute impossibility of reaching the lofty site of these depositions, was still there. Not an article of new furniture was added, while the old furniture looked more miserable and scanty, on account of some of the best pieces having been taken out to fill the cottage.

Dymock walked through the old circular hall, the ground-floor of the Tower, and went up the stairs to the room where Mrs. Margaret used to sit and darn in solitary state; there was the oriel window, which hanging over the moat, commanded a glorious view on three sides. Dymock walked up to this window, and stood in the oriel, endeavouring, if possible, to understand what the feelings of his ancestors might have been, when they could look from thence, and call all the lands their own as far as the border, without counting many broader and fairer fields, in the southern direction.

Whilst waiting there in deep and melancholy mood, suddenly his eye fell on the airy figure of Tamar standing on the opposite side of the moat, and looking up to him; as soon as she caught his eye, she kissed her hand and waved it to him, and well he could comprehend the sparkling smile which accompanied this motion, though he was too far off to see it. "And art thou not fair Maid of Judah," said the affectionate genius, "worth to me all the broad lands of my fathers? Could they purchase for me such love as thine? Art thou not the little ewe lamb of the poor man?—but none shall ever have thee from me my daughter, but one entirely worthy of thee?"

Scarcely had Dymock returned the courtesy of Tamar, before Jacob, who had run to the top of the Tower before him, came to tell him that his master was ready to see him, and Dymock, who needed no guide, soon found himself at the head of several more rounds of stairs, which got narrower as they ascended,—and in front of a narrow door well studded with knobs of iron. Within this door was a room, which in time past had been used for security, either for prisoners, treasures, or other purposes,—tradition said not what,—but it still had every requisite of strength, the narrow windows being provided with stauncheons of iron, and the walls covered with strong wainscotting, in one side of which were sliding pannels opening into a closet. The secret of these pannels was known only to Dymock, and he, when he sold the castle, had revealed it to Mr. Salmon, vaunting the great service of which this secret closet, had been, in keeping plate and other valuables, though he acknowledged, poor man, that he had never made any great use of this mysterious conservatory.

It seems that Mr. Salmon had appropriated this same room to his especial use; his bed, which in the French taste was covered with a tent-like tester, occupied one nook, and the curtains, as well as the floor-cloth, were of very rich, but tarnished and threadbare materials. Several ponderous tomes in vellum emblazoned with gold, were placed on a ledge of the wall near the bed; a square table, a trunk strongly clamped with brass, and an old fashioned easy chair, completed the furniture.

And now for the first time Dymock saw Mr. Salmon in his deshabille. The old gentleman had laid aside his coat, probably that it might be spared unnecessary wear and tear; he wore a claret coloured waistcoat with large flaps, on which were apparent certain tarnished remains of embroidery; his lower extremities, as far as the knees, were encased in a texture the colour of which had once been pepper and salt, and from the knee downwards he wore a pair of

Mrs. Sherwood

home-manufactured, grey worsted stockings, which proved that his housekeeper was by no means inferior to Mrs. Margaret in her darning talents, though we must do the Laird's aunt the justice to assert, that she never darned stockings with more than three different colours.

His slippers, both sole and upper part, had evidently at one time formed a covering of a floor, though what the original pattern and colours had been, could not now be made out. With all this quaintness of attire, the old man had the general appearance of neatness and cleanliness, and had it not been for the expression of his countenance, would have been far from ill-looking.

He received Dymock with a sort of quiet civility, not unlike that which a cat assumes when she is aware of a mouse, and yet does not perceive that the moment is come to pounce upon it. Dymock drew near to the table, and accosted Mr. Salmon with his usual courteous, yet careless manner, and having apologized for coming at all on such an errand, wishing that there was no such thing as money in the world, he presented the inconclusive and inefficient memorandum, which the old gentleman had given him, "trusting, as he said, that it would be no inconvenience for him to pay what he conceived would be a mere trifle to him."

Mr. Salmon had, it seems, forgotten to ask Dymock to sit down; indeed, there was no chair in the room but that occupied by his own person; however, he took his own note from the Laird's hands, and having examined it, he said, "But Mr. Dymock, there are conditions,—the memorandum is conditional, and I understand thereby, that I undertake to pay such and such moneys for such and such articles."

"Well Sir, and have you not these articles in possession?" asked Dymock; have I removed a single item, which I told you on the honour of a gentleman should be yours on such and such conditions, and did you not tell me that you would pay me a certain sum, on entering into possession of these articles?"

"What I did say, Sir," replied the old man, "is one thing; or rather what you choose to assert that I did say, and what is written here is another thing."

"Sir!" replied Dymock, "Sir! do you give me the lie?—direct or indirect, I will not bear it; I, a son of the house of Dymock, to be thus bearded in my own Tower, to be told that what I choose to assert may not be true; that I am, in fact, a deceiver,—a sharper,—one that would prevaricate for sordid pelf!" What more the worthy man added, our history does not say, but that he added much cannot be disputed, and that he poured forth in high and honourable indignation, many sentiments which would have done credit both to the gentleman and the Christian.

In the meantime the old man had drawn a huge bunch of keys from his pocket, and had deliberately opened the trunk before mentioned, at the top of which were sundry yellow canvass bags of specie; he next fitted a pair of spectacles on his nose, and then raising the cover of the table, he drew out a drawer containing a pair of scales, and began to weigh his guineas, as if to make a show of that of which he had none,—honesty; and the Laird having spent his indignation, was become quiet, and stood looking on, in a somewhat indolent and slouching attitude, making no question but that his honourable reasonings had prevailed, and that Mr. Salmon was about, without further hesitation, to pay him the five hundred and ninety-four pounds, ten shillings, and sixpence, which were his just due.

Whilst Salmon went on with this process of weighing, which

Mrs. Sherwood

he did with perfect *sang-froid*, he began to mutter. "Five hundred and ninety-four pounds, ten shillings, and six-pence; too much, too much by half, for worm-eaten bed-steads and chairs, darned curtains and faded portraits; but Mr. Dymock, to show you that I am a man of honour, I will pay you at this moment four hundred pounds in the King's gold, and the remainder, that is, the one hundred and ninety-four pounds, ten shillings, and six-pence, shall be put to arbitration; we will go over each item, you and I, and a friend of each, and we will examine every article together, and if it is decided that the things are worth the moneys, well and good, it shall be so, and I will forthwith pay down the residue, though not compelled so to do by bond or signature."

Again the hot blood of the Dymocks rose to the brow of the Laird; by an amazing effort of prudence and presence of mind, however, he caught up Salmon's note from the table, a motion which made the old man start, look up, and turn yellow, and then whisking round on his heel, with an expression of sovereign contempt, the Laird turned out of the room, exclaiming, "I scorn to address another word to thee, old deceiver; I shake the dust of thy floor from my foot; I shall send those to talk with thee, whose business it is to deal with deceivers;" and thus he quitted the chamber, drawing the door after him with a force which made every chamber in the Tower reverberate.

In descending the spiral stairs, he came to a narrow window, which overlooked the moat, and from thence he saw Tamar lingering on the other side thereof. He stood a moment and she called to him; her words were these,—"Have you sped?" in reply to which, protruding his head through the narrow aperture, he said: "No! the man's a low and despicable deceiver," adding other terms which were by no means measured by the rules of prudence or even courtesy; these words were not, however, lost on Tamar, and by what she then heard, she was induced to take a measure which had she deliberated longer thereon, she might not have ventured upon.

Dymock having spent his breath and his indignation through the window, to the disturbance of sundry bats and daws, which resided in the roof of the Tower, was become so calm that he made the rest of his descent in his usually tranquil and sluggish style, and even before he had crossed the court towards the draw-bridge, he had made up his mind to get Shanty to settle this knotty business, feeling that the old blacksmith would have been the proper person to have done it from the first.

Jacob, the ugly, ill-conditioned serving-man, was waiting to turn the light bridge, and had Dymock looked upon him, he would have seen that there was triumph on the features of this deformed animal, for Jacob was in all his master's secrets; he knew that he meant to cheat the Laird, and he being Salmon's foster brother, already counted upon his master's riches as his own. Salmon's constitution was failing rapidly, and Jacob, therefore, soon hoped to gather in his golden harvest.

Jacob too, hated every creature about him, and his hatred being inherited from his parents, was likely to be coeval with his life. The cause of this hatred will be seen in the sequel; but Jacob had no sooner turned the bridge and fixed it against the opposite bank, than Tamar springing from behind a cluster of bushes, jumped lightly on the boards, and the next moment she was with Dymock and Jacob on the inner side of the moat, under the tower.

Jacob had started back, as if he had seen a spectre, at the appearance of the blooming, sparkling Tamar, who came forward without hat or other head dress, her raven tresses floating in the breeze.

"Why are you here, my daughter?" said Dymock.

"Do not restrain me, dear father," she answered, "you have not sped you say, only permit me to try my skill;" and then turning suddenly to Jacob, she drew herself up, as Dymock would have said, like a daughter of kings, and added, "show me to your master, I have business with him; go and tell him that I am here, and that I would see him."

"And who are you?" asked Jacob, not insolently as was his wont, but as if under the impression of some kind of awe; "who shall I say you are?"

Dymock was about to answer; but Tamar placed her hand playfully on his lips, and took no other notice of the question of the serving man, but by repeating her command.

"What are you doing,—what do you propose to do, Tamar?" said the Laird. Tamar was fully aware that she had power to cause her patron at any time, to yield to her caprices; and she now used this power, as women know so well how to effect these things—not by reason—or persuasion, but by those playful manoeuvrings, which used in an evil cause have wrought the ruin of many a more steadfast character than Dymock.

"I have a thought dear father," she said, "a wish, a fancy, a mere whim, and you shall not oppose me: only remain where you are; keep guard upon the bridge, I shall not be absent long, only tell me how it has happened that your errand here has failed, and you," she added, addressing Jacob, "go to your master and tell him I am here."

"Why do you stand?" she added, stamping her little foot with impatience; "why do you not obey me?" and her dark eyes flashed and sparkled, "go and tell your master that I wish to see him."

"And who must I tell him that you are?" he asked.

"My name has been mentioned in your presence," she replied, "and if you did not hear it the fault is your own; it will not be told again."

"Are you the daughter of this gentleman?" asked Jacob.

"You have heard what he called me," she answered, "go and deliver my message."

Whilst Jacob was gone, for go he did, at the young girl's bidding, Dymock told Tamar all that had taken place in Mr. Salmon's room, and Tamar confessed her wish to be permitted to speak to the old gentleman herself. Dymock was glad that any one should undertake this business, provided he could be relieved from it, and he promised Tamar that he would stand by the bridge and watch for her till her return.

"Then I will myself go up to the Tower and demand admission:" so saying, she ran from Dymock, coursed rapidly through the various courts, and swift as the wind ascended the stairs, meeting no one in her way. She found the door of Salmon's chamber ajar, and pushing it open, she entered, and stood before Salmon, Jacob, and Rebecca (the old woman before mentioned as having come with Mr. Salmon to the Tower;) these three were all deep in consultation, Mr. Salmon being still seated where the Laird had left him.

As Tamar burst upon them in all the light of youth; of beauty, and of conscious rectitude in the cause for which she

Mrs. Sherwood

came, the three remained fixed as statues, Jacob and Rebecca in shrinking attitudes, their eyes set fearfully upon her, their faces gathering paleness as they gazed; whilst Salmon flushed to the brow, his eyes distended and his mouth half open.

The young girl advanced near to the centre of the room and casting a glance around her, in which might be read an expression of contempt quite free from fear, she said, "I am come by authority to receive the just dues of the late possessor of this place, and I require the sum to be told into my hand, and this I require in the name of Him who rules on high, and who will assuredly take cognizance of any act of fraud used towards a good and honourable man."

"And who? and who?" said Salmon, his teeth actually chattering "who are you? and whence come you?"

"I come from the Laird of Dymock," she answered, "and in his name I demand his rights!"

"You, you," said Salmon, "you are his daughter?"

"That remains to be told," replied Tamar, "what or who I am, is nothing to you, nor to you, nor you," she added, looking at Jacob and Rebecca, her eye being arrested for a minute on each, by the singular expression which passed over their countenances. "Give me the Laird's dues and you shall hear no more from me," she said, "never again will I come to trouble your dulness; but, if you deny it to me, you shall never rest from me;—no, no, I will haunt you day and night," and getting hotter as she continued to speak, "you shall have no rest from me, neither moat nor stone walls shall keep me out." She was thinking at that moment of the secret passage by which she fancied she might get into the Tower, if at this time she did not succeed; it was a wild and girlish scheme, and whether practicable or not, she had no time to think. As she uttered these last words, Salmon rose slowly from his seat, pushed his chair from behind him and stepped back, a livid paleness covering his features whilst he exclaimed: "Are you in life? or are you a terrible vision of my fancy? Jacob,—Rebecca,—do you see it too—Ah! you look pale, as those who see the dead—is it not so?"

The terror now expressed in the three countenances, was rapidly extending to the heart of Tamar. What can all this mean, she thought, what is there about me that thus appals them: it is their own guilt that renders them fearful; but why should I fear? now is the moment for strength of heart, and may heaven grant it to me. Having strength given her; she again demanded the just due of her guardian.

"It would be better to give it," muttered Jacob; and Rebecca at the same time screached out, "In the name of our father Abraham, give her what she asks, master,—and let her go,—let her go to her father,—to him that has reared her, and yet disowns her,—let her go to him; or like the daughters of Moab she will bring a curse on our house."

"Hold your tongue, you old fool," said Jacob, "what do you know of her, and of him who was once Laird of Dymock? But, master," he added "pay the girl what she asks, and I will go down and get back your note, and once for all we will shut our doors upon these people."

"But I would know," said Salmon, "I would know whence that girl has those eyes, which are bright as the bride of Solomon,—as Rachel's," he added, "they are such as hers."

"Go to," said Jacob, "what folly is this, tell the money to the girl, and let her go."

"Jacob! Jacob!" exclaimed Salmon, "I am ruined, undone, I shall come to beggary,—five hundred and ninty-four pounds, ten shillings and sixpence," and the teeth of the old man began to chatter, terror and dotage and cunning, seeming to be striving within him for the mastery and altogether depriving him of the power of acting.

Jacob muttered one or two indistinct imprecations, then approaching the table himself, he told the gold from the bags with the facility of a money-changer, whilst Tamar stood calmly watching him; but the serving man finding the weight too great for her, he exchanged much of the gold, for Bank of England notes, which he took out of the same trunk, and then delivering the sum into Tamar's hands; "There young woman, go," he said, "and never again disturb my master with your presence."

Whilst this was going on, Salmon had kept his eyes fixed on Tamar, and once or twice had gasped as if for breath; at length he said, "And you are Dymock's daughter, damsel, but you are not like your father's people,—are they not Nazarenes; tell me what was she who bore you?"

"Beshrew you," exclaimed Jacob, "what is all this to you," and roughly seizing Tamar by the arm, he drew her out of the room, saying, "you have all you want, go down to your father, and let us see you no more."

The young girl almost doubted as she descended the stairs, but that still she was over-reached, and if so, that Dymock would not perhaps find it out till it might be too late; she therefore, hearing Jacob behind her, ran with all her might, and coming to the place where Dymock stood, she called to him to follow her, and ran directly to Shanty's shed; Dymock proceeded after her a few yards behind, and Jacob still farther in the rear, crying "Laird, stop! stop! Mr. Dymock!

give us your release, here is a paper for you to sign."

Fortunately, Tamar found Shanty alone in his shed, and taking him into his inner room, she caused him to count and examine the money and thus was he occupied when Dymock and Jacob came in. Tamar went back to the outer room of the shed; but Shanty remained within, and when he found that all was right, Mr. Dymock gave his release. Jacob returned to the Tower, and old Shanty trotted off to Hexham, to put the money in a place of security; nor did he fail in his object, so that before he slept, the Laird had the satisfaction to think that this dirty work was all completed, and that without his having in the least soiled his own hands in the process. As to the mystery of Tamar's having been enabled to effect what he could not do, he soon settled that matter in his own mind, for, thought he, "if I the Laird of Dymock could never refuse a favour asked me by this maid of Judah, how could inferior minds be expected to withstand her influence?"—the poor Laird not considering that the very inferiority and coarseness of such minds as he attributed to Salmon and Jacob, would have prevented them from feeling that influence, which he had found so powerful. But they had felt something, which certainly belonged to Tamar, and had yielded to that something; nor could Tamar herself, when she reflected upon that scene in the Tower, at all comprehend how she had excited such emotions as she witnessed there; neither could Shanty, nor Mrs. Margaret help her out.

Again for another month, all went on in its usual routine; all was quiet at Dymock's Tower, and darning, writing, and hammering, continued to be the order of the day with Mrs. Margaret, the Laird, and Shanty, whilst Tamar was all gay and happy in the fulfilment of many active duties, rising with the lark, and brushing the dew from the frequent herbs which encompassed her dwelling. It was all summer with her then, nor did she spoil the present by anticipation of the severities of a wintery day, for the work of grace was going on with her, and though her natural temper was lofty and violent, as appeared by her manner to Jacob on the occasion lately described, yet there was a higher principle imparted, which rendered these out-breakings every day more rare.

We have said before, that Mrs. Margaret had a favourite cow, named by her mistress, Brindle, from the colours of her coat. Tamar had learned to milk Brindle, and this was always her first work. One morning in the beginning of August, it happened, or rather, was so ordered by Providence, that the Laird was constrained through the extreme activity of his imagination, which had prevented him from sleeping after midnight, to arise and go down to his study in order to put these valuable suggestions on paper. It was, however, still so dark when he descended into his study, that he was compelled to sit down awhile in his great chair, to await the break of day; and there that happened to him, which might as well have happened in bed,—that is he fell asleep, and slept soundly for some hours. All this, however, had not been done so quietly, but that he had awakened his sister and Tamar, who slept in the adjoining room; the consequence of which was, that Tamar got up and dressed herself, and having ascertained the situation of the Laird, and informed Mrs. Margaret that all was well in that quarter, she descended again into the kitchen, and proceeded to open the house-door. The shades of night were as yet not dispersed, although the morning faintly dawned on the horizon; but the air was soft, fragrant, and elastic, and as it filled the chest of Tamar, it seemed to inspire her with that sort of feeling, which makes young things whirl, and prance, and run, and leap, and perform all those antics which seem to speak of naught but folly to all the sober and discreet elders, who have forgotten that they were ever young.

Almost intoxicated with this feeling inspired by the morning air, Tamar bounded from the step of the door, and ran a considerable way, first along the bottom of the glen, and then in a parallel line on the green side thereof; suddenly coming to a stand, she looked for Brindle, and could not at first discern her; a minute afterwards, however, she saw her at the higher end of the glen, just where it opened on the moor, and where it had hitherto been protected from the inroads of the sheep, or other creatures feeding on the common, by a rail and gate. This rail and gate had wanted a little repair for several weeks, the Laird having promised to give it that repair; and he was well able so to have done, having at one time of his life worked several months with the village carpenter. But the good man had not fulfilled his promise, and it had only been the evening before that Tamar had tied up the gate with what came nearest to her hand, namely, certain tendrils of a creeper which hung thereabouts from the rock that formed the chasm by which the valley was approached in that direction. These tendrils she had twisted together so as to form a band, never supposing that Brindle, though a young and female creature, could possibly be sufficiently capricious to leave her usual fragrant pasturage, in order to pull and nibble this withering band. But, however, so it was, as Tamar asserted, for there when she came up to the place, the band was broken, the gate forced open, and Brindle walking quietly forward through the narrow gully towards the moor.

Tamar being come to the gate, stopped there, and called Brindle, who knew Tamar as well as she knew her own calf. But the animal had snuffed the air of liberty which came pouring down the little pass, from the open moor, and she walked deliberately on with that air which seemed to say,— "I hear your voice, but I am not coming."

Tamar was provoked; had it been a human creature who was thus acting she might perhaps have recollected that it is not good to give way to anger; as it was, she made no such reflection, but exclaiming in strong terms against the creature, she began to run, knowing that if Brindle once got on the moor it would probably cost her many a weary step before she could get her back again. In measure however, as she quickened her pace, so did Brindle, and in a few minutes the truant animal had reached the open moor and began to career away in high style, as if rejoicing in the trouble she was giving.

But even on the open moor it was yet very dusk; the dawn was hardly visible on the summits of the distant hills, and where there were woods or valleys the blackness was unbroken.

Tamar stood almost in despair, when she found that the animal had reached the open ground; but whilst watching how she could get round her, so as to turn her back, the creature rather slackened her pace, and began to browze the short grass among the heather. Tamar now slowly advancing was taking a compass to come towards her head, when she, perceiving her, turned directly round, and trotted on straightforward to the knoll, which was at most not half a quarter of a mile from the dingle; Tamar followed her, but could not reach her till she had pushed her way in among the trees and bushes, and when Tamar reached the place, she found her quietly feeding in the green area, surrounded by the ruins. The light was still very imperfect, and Tamar was standing half hid by the bushes and huge blocks of granite, doubting whether she should not leave the cow there whilst she ran back to call the Laird to assist her, when suddenly she was startled by the sound of voices. She drew closer behind the block, and remained perfectly still, and ceased to think of the cow, so great was her amazement to find persons in a place, generally deserted by the country people, under the impression that things were there which should not be spoken of. She then also remembered her adventure with Sappho, and what Mrs. Margaret had told her of the concealed passage; and now recollecting that secret passage, she was aware that she stood not very far from the mysterious door-way.

All these thoughts crowded to her mind, but perfect quiet was needful at the moment. As the disk of the sun approached the horizon, the light was rapidly increasing; the dawn in those higher latitudes is however long, but those who knew the signs of the morning were aware that it would soon terminate, and that they whose deeds feared the light had no time to lose.

Tamar accordingly heard low voices, speaking, as it were in the mouth of the cavern, and then a voice of one without the cavern—of one as in the act of departing, saying distinctly, "twelve then at midnight!" The answer from within did not reach Tamar's ears, at least, she heard only an indistinct murmur, but the voice without again came clear to her, and the words were to this effect, "I will not fail; I will take care that he shall be in no condition to return;" the answer was again lost to Tamar, and probably some question, but the reply to this question was clear. "It is his day to go,—the garrison can't live without provision,—if he don't go to-day, we must skulk another twenty-four hours,—we must not venture with him, there will be murder!" then followed several sentences in such broad slang, as Tamar could not comprehend, though she thought she understood the tendency of these words, which were mixed with oaths and terms so brutal, that her blood ran cold in thinking of them; "Caught in his own snare,—he will sink in his own dyke,— we have him now, pelf and all." After this, Tamar heard parting steps, and various low rumbling noises as if proceeding from under ground; then all was still, and no farther sound was heard by her, but the rustling of leaves, the chirping of birds, and the cropping of the herb by the incisors of Brindle. In the mean time the morning broke, the light of day was restored, and Tamar creeping gently from her hiding-place, left Brindle, whilst she ran back to the cottage.

She had not gone far, before she met the labourer who was accustomed to assist her in the care of the garden. She told him that the cow had strayed to the knoll, and that she had seen her enter among the trees; and he undertook, with his dog, to drive her back to the glen, though, he said, he would on no account go up on the knoll, but his dog would drive her down, and he would see her home.

"And why not go on to the knoll?" said Tamar. The man replied, that the place was known to be uncanny, and that not only strange noises, but strange sights had been seen there.

"Lately?" asked Tamar, "have they been seen and heard lately?"

The poor man could not assert that they had, and Tamar was not going to tell him what she had seen and heard. No! this mystery was to be left for the consideration of Dymock and Shanty, and she was anxious to know if their thoughts agreed with hers.

When she arrived at the cottage, and the labourer had brought back Brindle, and fastened the gate, and Tamar had milked her cow, and done her usual services, she went to Dymock who was just awake, and brought him out to breakfast with Mrs. Margaret, "You shall not say any thing about posterity, and the benefits which you are doing to them by recording your thoughts, this morning, sir," she said, "but you shall hear what I have to tell you, and I will not tell you, but in the presence of Mrs. Margaret." When Dymock heard what Tamar had to say, he was at first quite amazed, for it seems, that if he had ever heard of the secret passage he had forgotten it, and Mrs. Margaret had had her reasons, for not stirring up his recollections; but when he was made acquainted with this fact, and had put together all that Tamar had related, he made the same reflections which she had done, and said that he had no doubt, but that these ruins had been the rendezvous of vagrants for years, and that there was now a plan to rob Mr. Salmon, through the means of the secret passage. He went further, for he had no lack of imagination, and proceeded to conjecture, that it was through the manoeuvreing of these very vagrants, that the old curmudgeon had been brought to Dymock's Tower, and following the connexion, he began to put together the appearance of the young blacksmith, the gipsy who had left Tamar at Shanty's, her second appearance and rapid disappearance, the coming of Mr. Salmon, his supposed riches, his strange whim of shutting himself up, and every other extraordinary circumstance, in a jumble even more inexplicable and confusing, than any of his previous speculations upon these events,—and when he had so done he put on his hat, and declared that he must go forthwith to Shanty.

"To see," said Tamar, "what he can hammer out of it all, but something must and ought to be done to put Mr. Salmon on his guard, for otherwise, assuredly he will be robbed this night."

"And perhaps murdered," exclaimed Mrs. Margaret; "but go, brother, be quick, and let us have Shanty's advice."

"And I," said Tamar, after the Laird was departed, "will go to the Tower, and if possible get admittance. I will stop the going off of Jacob."

Mrs. Margaret expostulated with her, but all her pleadings came to this,—that she should send a neighbour to watch for

Tamar on the side of the moat, the young girl having assured her kind protectress, that she had nothing to fear for her, and that as the Laird was proverbially a procrastinator, he might let half the day pass, before he had settled what was to be done.

Poor Mrs. Margaret was all tremor and agitation; at the bottom of her heart, she did not like to be left in the cottage, so near a gang of thieves as she felt herself to be; she was not, however, a selfish character, and after some tears, she kissed Tamar and bade her go, watching her the whole way through the glen, as if she were parting with her for years.

The light step of the young girl, soon brought her to the edge of the moat, and she arrived, as it was ordered by Providence, at a very convenient time, for she met Rebecca on the moor, the old woman having just parted from Jacob, whose figure was still to be seen jogging along the heath. The first words of Tamar were to entreat Rebecca to call Jacob back, and when she found that she was speaking to one who chose to lend a deaf ear, she raised her own voice, but with equal ill success; turning then again to Rebecca, she saw that she was hastening to the bridge, on which she followed her, and was standing with her under the Tower, before the old woman could recollect herself.

The creature looked yellow with spite, as she addressed the young maiden with many bitter expressions, asking her what she did there, and bidding her to be gone.

"I am come," replied Tamar, "to see your master, and I will see him."

"It is what you never shall again," replied the dame; ' he has never been himself since he last saw you."

"How is that?" said Tamar; "What did I do, but press him to act as an honourable man, but of this I am resolved," she added, "that I will now see him again," and as she spoke, she proceeded through the postern into the courts, still passing on towards the principal door of the Tower, Rebecca following her, and pouring upon her no measured abuse. Tamar, however, remarked, that the old woman lowered her voice as they advanced nearer the house, on which she raised her own tones, and said, "I must, and will see Mr. Salmon, it is a matter of life and death I come upon;—life and death I repeat, and if you or your master, have any thing on your minds or consciences, you will do well to hear what I have to tell you; a few hours hence and it will be too late."

"In that case," said Rebecca, looking at one angry and terrified, "come with me, and I will hear you."

"No," exclaimed Tamar, speaking loud, "I will see your master, my errand is to him," and at the same instant, the quick eye of the young girl, observed the face of Salmon peering through a loop-hole, fitted with a casement, which gave light to a closet near the entrance. Encouraged by this she spoke again, and still louder than before, saying, "See him I will, and from me alone, shall he hear the news I am come to tell." The next minute she heard the casement open, and saw the head of the old man obtruded from thence, and she heard a querulous, broken voice, asking what was the matter? Tamar stepped back a few paces, in order that she might have a clearer view of the speaker, and then looking up, she said, "I am come Mr. Salmon as a friend, and only as a friend, to warn you of a danger which threatens you,—hear me, and you may be saved,—but if you refuse to hear me, I tell you, that you may be a ghastly livid corpse before the morning."

"Rebecca, Rebecca!" cried the old man, "Rebecca, I say,

Mrs. Sherwood

speak to her," and his voice faltered, the accents becoming puling.

"Hear her not," said the dame, "she is a deceiver, she is come to get money out of you."

"And heaven knows," cried Mr. Salmon, "that she is then coming to gather fruit from a barren tree. Money, indeed! and where am I to find money, even for her,—though she come in such a guise, as would wring the last drop of the heart's blood?"

"Tush!" said Rebecca, "you are rambling and dreaming again;" but the old man heard her not, he had left the lattice, and in a few seconds he appeared within the passage. During this interval, Rebecca had not been quiet, for she had seized the arm of Tamar, and the young girl had shaken her off with some difficulty, and not without saying, "Your unwillingness to permit me to speak to your master, old woman, goes against you, but it shall not avail you, speak to him I will," and the contest between Tamar and the old woman was still proceeding, when Salmon appeared in the passage.

Tamar instantly sprang to meet him, and seeing that his step was feeble and tottering, she supported him to a chair, in a small parlour which opened into the passage, and there, standing in the midst of the floor between him and Rebecca, she told her errand; nor was she interrupted until she had told all, the old man looking as if her recital had turned him into stone, and the old woman expressing a degree of terror, which at least cleared her in Tamar's mind, of the guilt of being connected with the thieves of the secret passage.

As soon as the young girl had finished, the old miser broke out in the most bitter and helpless lamentations. "My jewels! —my silver!—my moneys!" he exclaimed, "Oh my moneys!

—my moneys! Tell me, tell me damsel, what I can do? Call Jacob. Where is Jacob? Oh, my moneys!—my jewels!"

"Peace, good sir! peace!" said Tamar, "we will befriend you, we will assist you, we will protect you; the Laird is an honourable man, he will protect you. I have known him long, long,—since I was a baby; and he would perish before he would wrong any one, or see another wronged."

"The Laird did you say," asked Salmon, "your father; he is your father damsel is he not?"

"I have no other," replied Tamar, "I never knew another. Why do you ask me?"

"Because," said Rebecca, "he is doting, and thinks more of other people's concerns than his own."

"Has he ever lost a daughter?" asked Tamar.

"He lost a wife in her youth," answered the old woman, "and he was almost in his dotage when he married her, and he fancies because you have black hair, that you resemble her; but there is no more likeness between you two, than there is between a hooded crow and a raven."

"There is more though, there is much more though," muttered the old man, "and Jacob saw it too, and owned that he did."

"The fool!" repeated Rebecca, "the fool! did I not tell him that he was feeding your poor mind with follies; tell me, how should this poor girl be like your wife?"

The old man shook his head, and answered, "Because, he that made them both, fashioned them to be so; and Rebecca,

I have been thinking that had my daughter lived, had Jessica lived till now, she would have been just such a one."

"Preserve you in your senses, master," exclaimed Rebecca, "such as they are, they are better than none; but had your daughter lived, she would have been as unlike this damsel as you ever were to your bright browed wife. Why you are short and shrivelled, so was your daughter; your features are sharp, and so were hers; she was ever a poor pining thing, and when I laid her in her grave beside her mother, it was a corpse to frighten one; it was well for you, as I ever told you, that she died as soon."

"Yet had she lived, I might have had a thing to love," replied the old man; and then, looking at Tamar, he added, "They tell me you are the Laird's daughter,—is it so, fair maid?"

Rebecca again interrupted him. "What folly is this," she said, raising her voice almost to a shriek, "how know you but that, whilst you are questioning the damsel, your chests and coffers are in the hands of robbers; your money, I tell you, is in danger: your gold, your oft-told gold. You were not wont to be so careless of your gold; up and look after it. You will be reduced to beg your bread from those you hate; arise, be strong. Where are your keys? Give them to the damsel; she is young and active; she will swiftly remove the treasure out of the way. Can you not trust her? See you not the fair guise in which she comes? Can you suspect a creature who looks like your wife, like Rachel? Is not her tale well framed; and are you, or are you not deceived by her fair seemings? She is the daughter of a beggar, and she knows herself to be such; and there is no doubt but that she has her ends to answer by giving this alarm."

The old man had arisen; he looked hither and thither; he felt for his keys, which were hanging at his girdle; and then, falling back into his chair, he uttered one deep groan and became insensible, his whole complexion turning to a livid paleness.

"He is dying!" exclaimed Tamar, holding him up in his chair, from which he would have otherwise fallen. "He is dying, the poor old man is dying; bring water, anything."

"He has often been in this way since he came here," replied Rebecca. "We have thought that he has had a stroke; he is not the man he was a few months since; and had I known how it would be, it is strange but I would have found means to hinder his coming."

"If he were ever so before," said Tamar "why did you work him up, and talk to him, as you did, about his daughter; but, fetch some water," she added.

"I shall not leave him with you," answered Rebecca.

"Nor shall I abandon him to your tender mercies," replied Tamar, "whilst he is in this condition. I am not his daughter, it is true,—but he is a feeble old man, and I will befriend him if I can."

The old gentleman at this moment fell forward with such weight, that Tamar ran from behind him, and dropping down on her knees, received his head on her shoulder, then, putting one arm round him, she was glad to hear a long, deep sigh, the prelude of his returning to partial consciousness; and as he opened his eyes, he said,—"Ah, Rachel, is it you? You have been gone a long time."

Tamar was at that moment alone with the old man. Rebecca had heard voices at a distance, and she had run to pull up the bridge.

"I am not your Rachel, venerable Sir," she said; "but the adopted daughter of the Laird of Dymock," and she gently laid his head back.

"Then why do you come to me like her?" said the old man. "That is wrong, it is very cruel; it is tormenting me before my time. I have not hurt you, and I will give you more gold if you will not do this again."

"You rave, Sir," said Tamar. "Who do you take me for?"

"A dream," he answered. "I have been dreaming again;" and he raised himself, shook his head, rubbed his hands across his eyes, and looked as usual; but before he could add another word, Dymock and Shanty entered the parlour.

Rebecca had been too late in preventing their crossing the bridge, and they with some difficulty made the old gentleman understand that if he had any valuables, they must ascertain whether the place in which they were kept was any way approachable by the cavern. They also told him that they had taken means to have the exterior mouth of the cavern upon the knoll, stopped up, after the gang were in it; that they had provided a considerable force for this purpose; and that they should bring in men within the Tower to seize the depredators. Dymock then requested Tamar to return to Mrs. Margaret, and remain quietly with her; and when she was gone, the bridge was drawn up, and she went back to the cottage.

She had much to tell Mrs. Margaret, and long, very long,— after they had discussed many times the singular scene between Salmon, Rebecca, and Tamar, and spoken of what might be the plans of Dymock and Shanty for securing the Tower,—did the remainder of the day appear to them. Several times they climbed to the edge of the glen, to observe if aught was stirring; but all was still as usual. There stood the old Tower in solemn, silent unconsciousness of what might soon pass within it; and there was the knoll, looking as green and fresh as it was ever wont to do.

At sun-set Tamar and Mrs. Margaret again visited this post of observation, and again after they had supped at eight o'clock. They then returned and shut their doors; they made up their fires; and whilst Tamar plied her needle, Mrs. Margaret told many ancient tales and dismal predictions of secret murders, corpse-candles, and visions of second-sight, after which, as midnight approached, they became more restless and anxious respecting their friends, wondering what they would do, and expressing their hopes, or their fears, in dark sentences, such as these:—"We trust no blood may be shed!—if there should be blood!—if Dymock or poor Shanty should be hurt!" Again, they turned to form many conjectures, and put many things together:—"Was Mr. Salmon connected with the gipsies who had brought Tamar to the moor?—Was it this gang that proposed robbing him?—Was the young blacksmith called Harefoot connected with the gipsy?—Had he persuaded Salmon to bring his treasures there, in order that he might pilfer them?—And lastly, wherefore was Mr. Salmon so affected both times he had seen Tamar?" Here, indeed, was a subject for conjecture, which lasted some hours, and beguiled the sense of anxiety. At length the morning began to dawn on that long night, and Tamar went out to milk Brindle, whose caprices had, in fact, the day before, been the first mover in all this confusion. Cows must be milked, even were the master of the family dying; and Tamar wished to have this task over before any message should come from the Tower; and scarcely had she returned to the cottage, when the lad who administered the wind to Shanty's forge, came running with such haste, that, to use his own words,—"he had no more breath left for speaking than a broken bellows."

Mrs. Sherwood

"For the love of prince Charles," he said, "can you give us any provender, Mrs. Margaret? It is cold work watching all night, with neither food nor drink, save one bottle of whiskey among ten of us, and scarce a dry crust."

"But what have you done?" asked Tamar.

"We have nabbed them," replied the boy. "There were four of them, besides an old woman who was taken in the cave, and they are in the Tower till we can get the magistrates here, and proper hands to see them off. They came like rats from under ground. My master had made out where to expect them, in one of the cellars, behind the great hogshead which used to be filled at the birth of the heir, and emptied at his coming of age. So we were ready in the cellar, and nabbed three of them there, and the other, who was hindmost, and the woman, were taken as they ran out the other way; and there they are in the strong-hold, that is, the four men, but the woman is up above; and it is pitiful to hear how she howls and cries, and calls for the Laird; but he fell asleep as soon as he knew all was safe, and we have not the heart to disturb him."

"Well," said Mrs. Margaret, "I am most thankful that all is over without bloodshed, and my nephew asleep. No wonder, as he has not slept since twelve in the morning of yesterday."

"Excepting in his chair," said Tamar.

"But the provender, mistress," said the young man.

"Here," replied Tamar; "lift this pail on your head, and take this loaf, and I will follow with what else I can find."

"Nay, Tamar," said Mrs. Margaret, "You would not go where there is such a number of men and no woman, but that old witch Rebecca."

"I am not afraid of going where my father is," replied Tamar; "but I must see that woman. I should know her immediately. I am convinced that she is the very person who brought me to Shanty's shed. She hinted at some connexion with me. Oh, horrible! may it not be possible that I may have near relations among these miserable men who are shut up in the strong-hold of the Tower?"

As Tamar said these words, she burst into tears, and sunk upon the bosom of Mrs. Margaret, who, kissing her tenderly, said, "Child of my affections, of this be assured, that nothing shall separate you from me. My heart, methinks, clings more and more to you; and oh, my Tamar! that which I seem most to fear is that you should be claimed by any one who may have a right to take you from me."

This was a sort of assurance at that moment requisite to the poor girl; and such, indeed, was the interest which Mrs. Margaret felt in ascertaining if this really were the woman who had brought Tamar to Shanty's, that she put on her hood and cloak, and having filled a basket from the larder, she locked the cottage door, and went with Tamar to the Tower. It was barely light when they crossed the moat, for the bridge was not drawn; and when they entered the inner-court, they found many of the peasants seated in a circle, dipping portions of the loaf in Brindle's pail.

"Welcome! welcome! to your own place, Mrs. Margaret Dymock!" said one of them, "and here," he added, dipping a cup into the pail, "I drink to the restoration of the rightful heir and the good old family, and to your house-keeping, Mrs. Margaret; for things are done now in another style to what they were in your time."

Mrs. Sherwood

A general shout seconded this sentiment, and Mrs. Margaret, curtseying, and then pluming herself, answered, "I thank you, my friends, and flatter myself, that had my power been equal to my will, no hungry person should ever have departed from Dymock's Tower."

The ladies were then obliged to stand and hear the whole history of the night's exploit,—told almost in as many ways as there were tongues to tell it; and whilst these relations were going forward, the sun had fairly risen above the horizon, and was gilding the jagged battlements of the Tower.

Shanty was not with the party in the court, but he suddenly appeared in the door-way of the Tower. He seemed in haste and high excitement, and was about to call to any one who would hear him first, when his eye fell on Tamar and Mrs. Margaret. "Oh, there you are," he said; "I was looking for one of swift foot to bring you here. Come up this moment; you are required to be present at the confession of the gipsy wife, who is now willing to tell all, on condition that we give her her liberty. Whether this can be allowed or not, we doubt; though she did not make herself busy with the rest, but was caught as she tried to escape by the knoll."

"Oh! spare her, if possible," said Tamar, "or let her escape, if you can do nothing else to save her; I beseech you spare her!" Shanty made no reply, but led the way to an upper room of the Tower, which had in old time, when there were any stores to keep, (a case which had not occurred for some years,) been occupied as a strong-hold for groceries, and other articles of the same description; and there, besides the prisoner, who stood sullenly leaning against the wall, with her arms folded, sat Dymock and Salmon,—the Laird looking all importance, his lips being compressed and his arms folded,—and old Salmon, being little better in appearance than a *caput mortuum*, so entirely was the poor creature overpowered by the rapid changes in the scenes which were enacting before him.

Shanty had met Rebecca running down the stairs as he was bringing up Mrs. Margaret, and he had seized her and brought her in, saying, "Now old lady, as we are coming to a clearance, it might be just as well to burn out your dross among the rest; or may be," he added, "you may perhaps answer to the lumps of lime-stone in the furnace, not of much good in yourself, but of some service to help the smelting of that which is better,—so come along, old lady; my mind misgives me, that you have had more to do in making up this queer affair than you would have it supposed." The more Rebecca resisted, the more determined was Shanty; neither did he quit his hold of the old woman, until the whole party had entered the room, the door being shut, and his back set against it, where he kept his place, like a bar of iron in a stanchion.

Chairs had been set for Mrs. Margaret and Tamar, and when they were seated Dymock informed the prisoner that she might speak. Tamar had instantly recognized her; so had Shanty; and both were violently agitated, especially the former, when she began to speak. We will not give her story exactly in her own words; for she used many terms, which, from the mixture of gipsy slang and broad Border dialect, would not be generally understood; but, being translated, her narrative stood as follows:—

She was, it seems, of gipsy blood, and had no fixed habitation, but many hiding places, one of which was the cavern or passage connected with Dymock's Tower. Another of her haunts was Norwood Common, which, every one knows, is near London, and there was a sort of head-quarters of the gang, though, as was their custom, they seldom

Mrs. Sherwood

ccmmitted depredations near their quarters. She said, that, one day being on the common, she came in front of an old, black and white house, (which was taken down not many years afterwards;) in the front thereof was a garden, and a green lawn carefully trimmed, and in that garden on a seat sat an old lady, a tall and comely dame, she said, and she was playing with a little child, who might have been a year ard-a-half old. The gipsy, it seems, had asked charity through the open iron railing of the garden; and the lady had risen and approached the railing, bringing the child with her, ard putting the money into the infant's hand to pass it through the railing. The vagrant had then observed the dress and ornaments of the child, that she had a necklace of coral, clasped with some sparkling stone, golden clasps in her shoes, much rich lace about her cap, and above all, golden bracelets of curious workmanship on her wrists.

"She had not," said Rebecca; "she never wore those ornaments excepting on festival days."

The vagrant took no notice of this remark of Rebecca's; but Shanty gave the old servant a piercing look, whilst all others present, with the exception of Salmon, felt almost fainting with impatience; but Salmon's mind seemed for the moment in such a state of obtuseness, as disabled him from catching hold of the link which was leading to that which was to interest him as much as, or even more than, any one present. The gipsy went on to say, that her cupidity was so much excited by these ornaments, that she fixed her eye immediately on the family, and resolved, if possible, to get possession of the child. She first inquired respecting the family, and learned, that the house was occupied by a widow lady, who had with her an only daughter, a married woman; that the child she had seen belonged to that daughter; and that the husband was abroad, and was a Jew, supposed to be immensely rich.

"I knew it," said Dymock, turning round and snapping his fingers; "I hammered it out, Master Shanty, sooner than you did; I knew the physiognomy of a daughter of Zion at the very first glance; you, too, must never talk again of your penetration, Aunt Margaret," and the good man actually danced about the room; but Shanty on one side, and Aunt Margaret on the other, seized him by an arm, and forced him again upon his chair, entreating him to be still; whilst Salmon roused himself in his seat, shook off, or tried to shake off his confusion, and fixed his eyes stedfastly on the vagrant.

The woman then went on to describe the means by which she had got a sort of footing in this house; how she first discovered the back-door, and under what pretences she invited the servants to enter into a sort of concert with her for their mutual emolument, they bartering hare-skins, kitchen grease, cold meat, &c., for lace, tapes, thread, ballads, and other small matters.

"The thieves?" cried Salmon; but no one noticed him.

"There were only two servants in the house," said the gipsy; "there might be others, but I saw them not, and one of those now stands here;" and she fixed her eagle eye on Rebecca; "the other is Jacob."

"Jacob and Rebecca!" exclaimed Salmon; "it was my house, then, that you were robbing, and my servants whom you were tampering with."

"Go on," said Dymock to the vagrant, whose story then proceeded to this effect:—

She had visited the offices of this house several times; when, coming one evening by appointment of the servants, with some view to bartering the master's goods with her own wares, she found the family in terrible alarm, she had come as she said, just at the crisis in which a soul had parted, and it was the soul of that same old lady who had been playing with the infant on the grass-plot.

Rebecca was wailing and groaning in the kitchen, for she needed help to streak the corpse, and the family had lived so close and solitary, that she knew of no one at hand to whom to apply, and she feared that the dead would become stark and cold, before she could find help; Jacob was not within, he had gone to London, to fetch a Doctor of their own creed, and was not likely to be back for some time.

"And why? said I," continued the vagrant, "why, said I, should I not do for this service as well as another? for many and many had been the corpse which I had streaked; so she accepted my offer, and took me up to the chamber of death, and I streaked the body, and a noble corpse it was. The dame had been a comely one, as tall as that lady," pointing to Dymock's aunt, "and not unlike her."

"Ah!" exclaimed Mrs. Margaret, smiling, "I understand it now;" but Dymock bade her be silent, and the vagrant went on.

"So," said she, "when I had streaked the body, I said to Rebecca we must have a silver plate, for pewter will not answer the purpose."

"What for?" said she.

"'To fill with salt,' I answered, 'and set upon the breast.'"

"So she fetched me a silver plate half filled with salt, and I laid it on the corpse; 'and now,' I said, 'we must have rue and marjoram, run down and get me some;' and then I frightened her, poor fool as she was, by telling her that by the limpness of the hand of the corpse, I augured another death very soon in the house."

"When I told this to Rebecca, the creature was so frightened, that away she ran, leaving me in the room with the body. Swift as thought," continued the woman, "I caught the silver dish, and was running down stairs,—it was gloaming—when I saw a door open opposite the chamber of death, and there, in the glimmering, I saw the child of the family asleep in a little crib. She had on her usual dress, with the ornaments I spoke of, and seemed to have fallen asleep before her time, as she was not undressed. I caught her up, asleep as she was, and the next moment I was out in the yard, and across the court, and through the back-door, and away over the common, and to where I knew that none would follow me, but they of my people, who would help my flight."

"And the child with you," said Salmon, "did you take the child?"

"More I will not tell," added the woman; "no, nor more shall any tortures force from me, unless you bind yourselves not to prosecute me,—unless you promise me my liberty."

"I have told you," said the Laird, "that if you tell every thing you shall be free,—do you question my truth?"

"No, Dymock," said the vagrant; "I know you to be a man of truth, and in that dependence you shall hear all."

"I stripped the child of her gaudery, I wrapped her in rags, and I slung her on my back; but I did her no harm, and many a weary mile I bore her, till I came to the moor; and then, because she was a burden, and because the brand on her

Mrs. Sherwood

shoulder would assuredly identify her, if suspicion fell on me for having stolen her, I left her in the old blacksmith's shed, and there she found a better father than you would have made her; for what are you but a wicked Jew, with a heart as hard as the gold you love."

The fixed, and almost stone-like attitude in which the old man stood for some moments after his understanding had admitted the information given by the vagrant, so drew the attention of all present, that there was not a sound heard in the room, every one apprehending that the next moment they should see him drop down dead, nor did any one know what was best to do next; but this moment of terror was terminated by the old man's sinking on his knees, clasping his hands, and lifting his eyes, and breaking out in a short but solemn act of thanksgiving, and then turning his head without rising, as it were looking for his daughter, she sprang toward him, and threw her arms about him, whilst he still knelt. It would be difficult to describe the scene which followed: Dymock began to caper and exult, Mrs. Margaret to weep, Rebecca to utter imprecations, and Shanty to sing and whistle, as he was wont to do when hammering in his shed, and the vagrant to dare the old Jewess to deny any thing which she had said. When Dymock had assisted Tamar to lift her father into the chair, and when the old man had wept plentifully, he was again anxious to examine the case more closely; and a discussion followed, in which many things were explained and cleared up on both sides, though it was found necessary for this end, to promise Rebecca that she should be forgiven, and no vengeance taken upon her, if she should confess her part of the history. This discussion lasted long, and the substance of what was then opened to Tamar and her paternal friends was this:—Mr. Salmon was, it seems, a Polish Jew, extremely rich, and evidently very parsimonious; he had had mercantile concerns in London, and had there married, when nearly fifty years of age, a beautiful young

Jewess, whose mother he had greatly benefitted, when in the most deplorable circumstances. With this lady he had gone abroad, and it was very evident that he had been a severe and jealous husband. She had brought him a daughter soon after her marriage. This child was born in Poland, Rebecca was her nurse; but Mrs. Salmon, falling into bad health immediately after the birth of the child, she implored her husband to permit her to return to England, and to her mother. Salmon saw that she was not happy with him; and the strange suspicion seized him, as there was little tie between him and his wife, that in case his own child died, she might palm another upon him,—to prevent which, he branded the babe with the figure of a palm branch, and sent her home, with Rebecca and Jacob, who were both Jews, to watch her; though there was no need, as Rachel was a simple, harmless creature. She was also in very bad health when she reached England, and scarcely survived her mother three days, and during that time hardly asked for her child; and the artful servants had contrived to make their master believe that the baby had proved a sickly deformed creature, and had died, and been buried in the coffin with its mother.

Salmon was in Poland when all these horrors occurred, and there Jacob and Rebecca found him; and having now no other object, he devoted himself entirely to amassing riches, passing from one state of covetousness to another, till at length he began to fall into the dotage of avarice, which consists in laying up money for the sake of laying up, and delighting in the view of hoards of gold and precious things. With this madness in his mind, he turned much of his property into jewels, and returning to England, he began to look about for a safe place wherein he might deposit his treasures. But, as a Jew, he could not possess land; he therefore passed the form of naturalization, and whilst looking about for a situation in which he might dwell in safety, his character and circumstances became in part known to the gipsies, (who, amongst other thieves, always have their eyes on those who are supposed to carry valuables about them,) and the man called Harefoot, formed the plan of getting him and his treasures into Dymock's Tower. This Harefoot was the nephew of the woman who had brought Tamar to Shanty's; and the old miser, being tempted by the moat, and other circumstances of the place, fell into the snare which had been thus skillfully laid for him. It was not till after Salmon had come to the Tower, that the connection between Salmon and Tamar was discovered by the old woman; and it was at this time that she contrived to meet Tamar, and to convey the notion to her, that she was of a gipsy family; fearing lest she should, by any means, be led to an explanation with Salmon, before her nephew and his gang had made sure of the treasure. Harefoot had supposed that he and his gang were the only persons who knew of the secret passage; and the reason why they had not made the attempt of robbing Salmon by that passage sooner, was simply this, that Harefoot, having been detected in some small offence in some distant county, had been confined several weeks in a house of correction, from which he had not been set free many days before he came to the moor, and took upon himself the conduct of the plot for robbing Salmon.

What Jacob and Rebecca's plans were did not appear, or wherefore they had not only fallen in with, but promoted the settlement of their master in the Tower; but that their object was a selfish one cannot be doubted.

Had other confirmation been wanting, after the mark on Tamar's shoulder had been acknowledged, the vagrant added it, by producing a clasp of one armlet, which she had retained, and carried about with her in a leathern bag, amongst sundry other heterogeneous relics; and she accounted for having preserved it, from the fear she had of exposing a cypher wrought on a precious stone, which might, she thought, lead to detection.

A dreadful hue and cry in the court below, soon after this disturbed the conference. All seemed confusion and uproar; Dymock and Shanty rushed down stairs, and aunt Margaret and Tamar ran out to the window in the nearest passage; there they learnt that the prisoners had broken the bars of their dungeon, swam the moat, and fled; and the ladies could see the peasants in pursuit, scouring over the moor, whilst those they were pursuing were scarcely visible.

"I am glad of it," said Tamar, "I should rejoice in their escape, they will trouble us no more; and oh, my dear mother, I would not, that one sad heart, should now mix itself with our joyful ones!"

Mrs. Margaret and Tamar stood at the window till they saw the pursuers turning back to the castle, some of them not being sorry in their hearts, at the escape of the rogues, but the most remarkable part of the story was, that whilst they had all been thus engaged, the woman had also made off, and, though probably not in company with her, that most excellent and faithful creature Rebecca, neither of whom were ever heard of again.

And now none were left, but those who hoped to live and die in each other's company, but these were soon joined by the magistrates and legal powers, who had been summoned from the nearest town, together with people from all quarters, who flocked to hear and learn what was going forward; and here was an opportunity not to be lost by Dymock and Shanty, of telling the wonderful tale, and old Salmon having been recruited with some small nourishment, administered by Mrs. Margaret, presented his daughter to the whole assembly, and being admonished by Shanty, placed in her hands before them, the deed of transfer of the lands and castle of Dymock, which in fact to him, was but a drop in the ocean of his wealth.

As she received this deed, she fell on one knee, and kissed her venerable father's hand, after which he raised and embraced her, paternal affection and paternal pride acting like the genial warmth of the sun, in thawing the frost of his heart and frame. She had whispered something whilst he kissed her, and as his answer had been favourable, she turned to Dymock, and now bending on both knees, she placed the deed in his hands, her sweet face at the same time being all moist with gushing tears, falling upon her adopted father's hand.

Shanty in his apron and unshorn chin, explained to those about, what had been done; for they, that is the Laird, Aunt Margaret, Salmon, and Tamar, were standing on the elevated platform, at the door of the Tower: and then arose such shouts and acclamations from one and all, as made the whole castle ring again, and one voice in particular arose above the rest, crying, "Our Laird has got his own again, and blessing be on her who gave it him."

"Rather bless Him," cried Shanty, "who has thus brought order out of confussion, to Him be the glory given in every present happiness, as in all that we are assured of in the future."

As there were no means of regaling those present at that time, and as Mr. Salmon was then too confused to do that which he ought to have done, in rewarding those who had defended him, most of them being poor people, they were dismissed with an invitation to a future meeting at the Tower; two or three gentlemen, friends of Dymock, only being left. Much consultation then ensued, whilst Mrs. Margaret bestirred herself, to procure female assistance, and to provide the best meal, which could be had at a short notice.

During this conference with the Laird and his friends, all of whom were honourable men, Mr. Salmon was induced to consent to have his treasures, his bonds, his notes and bills, consigned to such keeping as was judged most safe; neither, could these matters be settled, without a journey to town, in which Dymock accompanied him, together with a legal friend of the latter of known respectability. We do not enter into the particulars of this journey, but merely say, that Mr. Salmon in the joy, and we may add, thankfulness of recovering his child, not only permitted himself to be advised, but whilst in town made his will, by which, he left all he possessed to his daughter, and this being concluded to the satisfaction of all concerned, he returned to Dymock's Tower, laden with presents for Mrs. Margaret.

Neither were Shanty's services overlooked; the cottage and land appertaining thereunto, were to be his for life, free from rent and dues, together with twenty pounds a year, in consideration of his never-varying kindness to Tamar.

The old man wept, when told of what was done for him, and himself went the next day to Morpeth, to bring from thence a sister, nearly as old as himself, who was living there in hard service.

And here the memorandum from which this story is derived, becomes less particular in the details.

It speaks of Mr. Salmon after the various exertions he had made, (these exertions having been as it was supposed succeeded by a stroke,) sinking almost immediately into a state nearly childish, during which, however, it was a very great delight to Tamar, to perceive in the very midst of this intellectual ruin an awakening to things spiritual; so that it would seem, as if the things hidden from him in the days of human prudence and wisdom, were now made manifest to him, in the period of almost second childishness.

Tamar had been enabled to imbibe the purest Christian principles, in her early youth, for which, humanly speaking, she owed much to Shanty, and she now with the assistance of the kind old man, laboured incessantly, to bring her father to the Messiah of the Christians, as the only hope and rest of his soul; and she had reason before her father died, to hope that her labours had not been without fruit. As to worldly pelf, she had it in rich abundance, but she could have little personal enjoyment of it whilst shut up with her aged father in Dymock's Tower, yet she had exquisite delight in humouring therewith, the fancies of Dymock, and administering to the more sober and benevolent plans of Mrs. Margaret; for this lady's principal delight was, to assist the needy, and her only earthly or worldly caprice, that of restoring the Tower and its environs, and furnishing, to what she conceived had been its state, in the, perhaps, imaginary days of the exaltation of the Dymocks.

A splendid feast in the halls of Dymock's Tower, is also spoken of, as having taken place, soon after the return of the Laird from London, from which, not a creature dwelling on the moor was absent, when Salmon directed Tamar to reward those persons who had assisted him in his greatest need, and when Mrs. Margaret added numbers of coats and garments to those that were destitute. Dymock in his joy of heart, caused the plough to be brought forward, and fixed upon a table in the hall, for every one to see that day, Mrs. Margaret having been obliged to acknowledge, that it was this same plough, which had turned up the vein of gold, in which all present were rejoicing.

With the notice of this feast the history terminates, and here the writer concludes with a single sentiment,—that although a work of kindness wrought in the fear of God, as imparted by the Lord, the Spirit—seldom produces such a manifest reward, as it did in the case of Mrs. Margaret and her nephew, for the race is not always to the swift, nor the burthen to the strong, yet, even under this present imperfect dispensation, there is a peace above all price, accompanying every act, which draws a creature out of self, to administer to the necessities of others, whenever these acts are performed in faith, and with a continual reference to the pleasure of God, and without view to heaping up merits, which is a principle entirely adverse to anything like a correct knowledge of salvation by the Lord the Saviour.

Choose from Thousands of 1stWorldLibrary Classics By

A. M. Barnard
Ada Leverson
Adolphus William Ward
Aesop
Agatha Christie
Alexander Aaronsohn
Alexander Kielland
Alexandre Dumas
Alfred Gatty
Alfred Ollivant
Alice Duer Miller
Alice Turner Curtis
Alice Dunbar
Allen Chapman
Alleyne Ireland
Ambrose Bierce
Amelia E. Barr
Amory H. Bradford
Andrew Lang
Andrew McFarland Davis
Andy Adams
Angela Brazil
Anna Alice Chapin
Anna Sewell
Annie Besant
Annie Hamilton Donnell
Annie Payson Call
Annie Roe Carr
Annonaymous
Anton Chekhov
Archibald Lee Fletcher
Arnold Bennett
Arthur C. Benson
Arthur Conan Doyle
Arthur M. Winfield
Arthur Ransome
Arthur Schnitzler
Arthur Train
Atticus
B.H. Baden-Powell
B. M. Bower
B. C. Chatterjee
Baroness Emmuska Orczy
Baroness Orczy
Basil King
Bayard Taylor
Ben Macomber
Bertha Muzzy Bower
Bjornstjerne Bjornson

Booth Tarkington
Boyd Cable
Bram Stoker
C. Collodi
C. E. Orr
C. M. Ingleby
Carolyn Wells
Catherine Parr Traill
Charles A. Eastman
Charles Amory Beach
Charles Dickens
Charles Dudley Warner
Charles Farrar Browne
Charles Ives
Charles Kingsley
Charles Klein
Charles Hanson Towne
Charles Lathrop Pack
Charles Romyn Dake
Charles Whibley
Charles Willing Beale
Charlotte M. Braeme
Charlotte M. Yonge
Charlotte Perkins Stetson
Clair W. Hayes
Clarence Day Jr.
Clarence E. Mulford
Clemence Housman
Confucius
Coningsby Dawson
Cornelis DeWitt Wilcox
Cyril Burleigh
D. H. Lawrence
Daniel Defoe
David Garnett
Dinah Craik
Don Carlos Janes
Donald Keyhoe
Dorothy Kilner
Dougan Clark
Douglas Fairbanks
E. Nesbit
E. P. Roe
E. Phillips Oppenheim
E. S. Brooks
Earl Barnes
Edgar Rice Burroughs
Edith Van Dyne
Edith Wharton

Edward Everett Hale
Edward J. O'Biren
Edward S. Ellis
Edwin L. Arnold
Eleanor Atkins
Eleanor Hallowell Abbott
Eliot Gregory
Elizabeth Gaskell
Elizabeth McCracken
Elizabeth Von Arnim
Ellem Key
Emerson Hough
Emilie F. Carlen
Emily Bronte
Emily Dickinson
Enid Bagnold
Enilor Macartney Lane
Erasmus W. Jones
Ernie Howard Pie
Ethel May Dell
Ethel Turner
Ethel Watts Mumford
Eugene Sue
Eugenie Foa
Eugene Wood
Eustace Hale Ball
Evelyn Everett-green
Everard Cotes
F. H. Cheley
F. J. Cross
F. Marion Crawford
Fannie E. Newberry
Federick Austin Ogg
Ferdinand Ossendowski
Fergus Hume
Florence A. Kilpatrick
Fremont B. Deering
Francis Bacon
Francis Darwin
Frances Hodgson Burnett
Frances Parkinson Keyes
Frank Gee Patchin
Frank Harris
Frank Jewett Mather
Frank L. Packard
Frank V. Webster
Frederic Stewart Isham
Frederick Trevor Hill
Frederick Winslow Taylor

Friedrich Kerst	Hayden Carruth	James Branch Cabell
Friedrich Nietzsche	Helent Hunt Jackson	James DeMille
Fyodor Dostoyevsky	Helen Nicolay	James Joyce
G.A. Henty	Hendrik Conscience	James Lane Allen
G.K. Chesterton	Hendy David Thoreau	James Lane Allen
Gabrielle E. Jackson	Henri Barbusse	James Oliver Curwood
Garrett P. Serviss	Henrik Ibsen	James Oppenheim
Gaston Leroux	Henry Adams	James Otis
George A. Warren	Henry Ford	James R. Driscoll
George Ade	Henry Frost	Jane Abbott
Geroge Bernard Shaw	Henry James	Jane Austen
George Cary Eggleston	Henry Jones Ford	Jane L. Stewart
George Durston	Henry Seton Merriman	Janet Aldridge
George Ebers	Henry W Longfellow	Jens Peter Jacobsen
George Eliot	Herbert A. Giles	Jerome K. Jerome
George Gissing	Herbert Carter	Jessie Graham Flower
George MacDonald	Herbert N. Casson	John Buchan
George Meredith	Herman Hesse	John Burroughs
George Orwell	Hildegard G. Frey	John Cournos
George Sylvester Viereck	Homer	John F. Kennedy
George Tucker	Honore De Balzac	John Gay
George W. Cable	Horace B. Day	John Glasworthy
George Wharton James	Horace Walpole	John Habberton
Gertrude Atherton	Horatio Alger Jr.	John Joy Bell
Gordon Casserly	Howard Pyle	John Kendrick Bangs
Grace E. King	Howard R. Garis	John Milton
Grace Gallatin	Hugh Lofting	John Philip Sousa
Grace Greenwood	Hugh Walpole	John Taintor Foote
Grant Allen	Humphry Ward	Jonas Lauritz Idemil Lie
Guillermo A. Sherwell	Ian Maclaren	Jonathan Swift
Gulielma Zollinger	Inez Haynes Gillmore	Joseph A. Altsheler
Gustav Flaubert	Irving Bacheller	Joseph Carey
H. A. Cody	Isabel Cecilia Williams	Joseph Conrad
H. B. Irving	Isabel Hornibrook	Joseph E. Badger Jr
H.C. Bailey	Israel Abrahams	Joseph Hergesheimer
H. G. Wells	Ivan Turgenev	Joseph Jacobs
H. H. Munro	J.G.Austin	Jules Vernes
H. Irving Hancock	J. Henri Fabre	Julian Hawthrone
H. R. Naylor	J. M. Barrie	Julie A Lippmann
H. Rider Haggard	J. M. Walsh	Justin Huntly McCarthy
H. W. C. Davis	J. Macdonald Oxley	Kakuzo Okakura
Haldeman Julius	J. R. Miller	Karle Wilson Baker
Hall Caine	J. S. Fletcher	Kate Chopin
Hamilton Wright Mabie	J. S. Knowles	Kenneth Grahame
Hans Christian Andersen	J. Storer Clouston	Kenneth McGaffey
Harold Avery	J. W. Duffield	Kate Langley Bosher
Harold McGrath	Jack London	Kate Langley Bosher
Harriet Beecher Stowe	Jacob Abbott	Katherine Cecil Thurston
Harry Castlemon	James Allen	Katherine Stokes
Harry Coghill	James Andrews	L. A. Abbot
Harry Houidini	James Baldwin	L. T. Meade

L. Frank Baum
Latta Griswold
Laura Dent Crane
Laura Lee Hope
Laurence Housman
Lawrence Beasley
Leo Tolstoy
Leonid Andreyev
Lewis Carroll
Lewis Sperry Chafer
Lilian Bell
Lloyd Osbourne
Louis Hughes
Louis Joseph Vance
Louis Tracy
Louisa May Alcott
Lucy Fitch Perkins
Lucy Maud Montgomery
Luther Benson
Lydia Miller Middleton
Lyndon Orr
M. Corvus
M. H. Adams
Margaret E. Sangster
Margret Howth
Margaret Vandercook
Margaret W. Hungerford
Margret Penrose
Maria Edgeworth
Maria Thompson Daviess
Mariano Azuela
Marion Polk Angellotti
Mark Overton
Mark Twain
Mary Austin
Mary Catherine Crowley
Mary Cole
Mary Hastings Bradley
Mary Roberts Rinehart
Mary Rowlandson
M. Wollstonecraft Shelley
Maud Lindsay
Max Beerbohm
Myra Kelly
Nathaniel Hawthrone
Nicolo Machiavelli
O. F. Walton
Oscar Wilde
Owen Johnson
P.G. Wodehouse
Paul and Mabel Thorne

Paul G. Tomlinson
Paul Severing
Percy Brebner
Percy Keese Fitzhugh
Peter B. Kyne
Plato
Quincy Allen
R. Derby Holmes
R. L. Stevenson
R. S. Ball
Rabindranath Tagore
Rahul Alvares
Ralph Bonehill
Ralph Henry Barbour
Ralph Victor
Ralph Waldo Emmerson
Rene Descartes
Ray Cummings
Rex Beach
Rex E. Beach
Richard Harding Davis
Richard Jefferies
Richard Le Gallienne
Robert Barr
Robert Frost
Robert Gordon Anderson
Robert L. Drake
Robert Lansing
Robert Lynd
Robert Michael Ballantyne
Robert W. Chambers
Rosa Nouchette Carey
Rudyard Kipling
Saint Augustine
Samuel B. Allison
Samuel Hopkins Adams
Sarah Bernhardt
Sarah C. Hallowell
Selma Lagerlof
Sherwood Anderson
Sigmund Freud
Standish O'Grady
Stanley Weyman
Stella Benson
Stella M. Francis
Stephen Crane
Stewart Edward White
Stijn Streuvels
Swami Abhedananda
Swami Parmananda
T. S. Ackland

T. S. Arthur
The Princess Der Ling
Thomas A. Janvier
Thomas A Kempis
Thomas Anderton
Thomas Bailey Aldrich
Thomas Bulfinch
Thomas De Quincey
Thomas Dixon
Thomas H. Huxley
Thomas Hardy
Thomas More
Thornton W. Burgess
U. S. Grant
Upton Sinclair
Valentine Williams
Various Authors
Vaughan Kester
Victor Appleton
Victor G. Durham
Victoria Cross
Virginia Woolf
Wadsworth Camp
Walter Camp
Walter Scott
Washington Irving
Wilbur Lawton
Wilkie Collins
Willa Cather
Willard F. Baker
William Dean Howells
William le Queux
W. Makepeace Thackeray
William W. Walter
William Shakespeare
Winston Churchill
Yei Theodora Ozaki
Yogi Ramacharaka
Young E. Allison
Zane Grey

www.ingramcontent.com/pod-product-compliance
Lightning Source LLC
Chambersburg PA
CBHW050804250626

47155CB00005B/2210